Praise for *T*

"What a refreshing perspective and immensely valuable offering! In her new book, *Soul Path Way*, Kay Taylor provides lucid, honest, and unpretentious spiritual guidance to access the core of our true calling. It seems obvious that she has twisted her ankles a few times, walking herself this path to self-realization, and has humor about our inevitable dramas. But as she weaves the path through the maze of life, drawing on the ancient wisdom of Astrology, Yogic philosophy, and Western spirituality, among other spiritual frameworks, Kay provides tangible tools to truly access the extraordinary—our individual Soul Destiny."
— Maurice Fernandez, author of *Astrology & the Evolution of Consciousness*

"In this book, Kay Taylor has developed her own vision of evolutionary astrology, presenting expansive meditation practices and spiritual teachings, conveyed with gentle humor and refreshing emotional honesty and truthfulness. Those who make the effort to transform themselves through Kay's guidance will feel richly rewarded as they come to a clearer understanding of their life's purpose and direction. Soul Path Way invites and inspires readers to embark upon an enlightening inner journey, where astrology becomes a vehicle for awakening."
—Greg Bogart, author of *Planets in Therapy* and *Astrology and Meditation: The Fearless Contemplation of Change*

"Kay Taylor is a clear and compassionate intuitive guide who has been a wonderful support for our family for many years. Her deep sense of knowing and her ability to articulate wisdom is precise, grounded and accurate. *Soul Path Way* brings real grounded guidance to heal, release and live life with a deep connection to the ever-present love of the divine. A gift we will share with many!"
—Lauren & Rick Allen, drummer of Def Leppard

"*Soul Path Way* brings us a wealth of wisdom—not the wisdom of a renunciate but of a spirituality integrated with the glories and challenges of the human experience. Having worked with Kay Taylor on my own soul path, healing and evolution for over fifteen years, I can attest that the inspiring and engaging words in this book are grounded in 'real living' and that the insights and guidance are authentic...If you have been looking for a fresh and powerful voice in the tradition of writers and inspirations like Wayne Dyer (who cherish and believe that we are 'infinite spiritual beings having temporary human experiences') look no further...*Soul Path Way* will help you to not only activate love in your life but to truly love your life!"
—Halfdan Hussey, co-founder & CEO of Cinequest

"Kay Taylor is a brilliant, intuitive and knowledgeable guide to soul's purpose. Her one-on-one work is vital, always encouraging and life-changing—helping us risk and dare and yet feel safe along the way. She has helped thousands of people in classes and sessions. Now we are blessed with her book reflecting years of study and practice—a gift to anyone seeking to understand who they are at the deepest levels, where they are in the world, and what they most need to do to live the fullest and most valuable life possible..."
—Susan G. Wooldridge, author of *poemcrazy*

"Kay Taylor has been an impeccable guide for me for over a decade and her uncanny inner sight is time and again confirmed by outer events. In short, Kay is a trustworthy healer, teacher and intuitive. This book is in Kay's warm, encouraging no-nonsense voice. I highly recommend it to people seeking a grounded and effective path to wholeness, who want to be divine and ordinary in equal measure."
—Vicki Robin, coauthor *Your Money or Your Life* and author of *Blessing the Hands That Feed Us*

Soul Path Way

The Dance of Astrology, Intuition & Spiritual Awakening

by Kay Taylor

Raven Dreams Press
Portland, OR

Published in 2016 by Raven Dreams Press
1434 NE Prescott St.
Portland, OR 97211
www.ravendreamspress.com

ISBN 978-0-9840474-6-8
LCCN: 2016946727

Cover Art Customization: Sara Fisk
Book design and production: Tony Howard & Eled Cernik

Printed in the United States of America

TABLE OF CONTENTS

(Infinite) Spaces.. xi
Acknowledgments....................................... xii
Preface xv
Foreword xix

Part One – Introduction

Prologue
Swan Vision 2

Chapter One
(Vegan) Duck Soup................................. 4

Chapter Two
Heart Clues.. 16

Chapter Three
Twelve Life Foundations........................... 23

Part Two – The Astrology of Soul Path

Chapter Four
The Evolutionary Story 32

Chapter Five
Pluto.. 65

Chapter Six
Saturn   70

Chapter Seven
Soul Path Mission Statement   74

Part Three – Four Pillars of Healing

Chapter Eight
Where do you Start? Perhaps Where You Are?.   80

Chapter Nine
The Spiritual Pillar   90

Chapter Ten
Spiritual/Meditation   99

Chapter Eleven
Intuition 109

Chapter Twelve
The Mental Pillar. 151

Chapter Thirteen
The Emotional Pillar. 164

Chapter Fourteen
The Physical Pillar. 180

Part Four – Manifestation & Co-Creation

Chapter Fifteen
Divine Creation 198

Chapter Sixteen
The Daily Plan 224

Chapter Seventeen
Beloveds & Tribe.................................... 230

Chapter Eighteen
Connection to the World........................... 242

Chapter Nineteen
Everyday Awakening: (Infinite) Soul Path............. 249

A List of Prominent Evolutionary Astrologers 258
Table of Nodes 260
Pluto Table 263
Saturn Table (Eastern Times)........................... 264
Reflections: Table of Meditations & Journal Exercises 268
Bibliography... 271
About the Author....................................... 274

(Infinite) Spaces

May the Creator of the Universe
Carve out all the contours
Of her imagination
And mine.
May the endless possibilities
Of what might be
Serve as the graceful release
Of what is.

May the Sustainer of the Universe
Sing aloud all the words
That make up her worlds
And mine.
May the music rebound and resound
In the sacred caves
Of what I am
And what I will be.

May the Destroyer of the Universe
Dance away all the fears
That limit her heart
And mine.
May the infinite spaces that hold us
Reverberate with the rhythm
Of our breathing
And the beat of our joy.

© Anasuya Sengupta
October 2015

ACKNOWLEDGMENTS

No one writes a book alone. Even in the cherished room of one's own. I bow deeply to all of my teachers, and to their teachers.

I thank my mentor and beloved friend Steven Forrest for holding the Capricorn torch to light my path, and for asking me Every Single Time he saw me (for years), "How's the book coming?" Plus, he pointed out that the fact I was working concurrently on several books would pretty much guarantee I would be published posthumously. So I allowed one book to surge forward and promise the others are following close behind. Joke well taken.

Gratitude to the precious Tony Howard for the ease and precision with which he does everything. Virgo on steroids, a wonderful publisher. Thank you Carol for your excellent edit support.

I am grateful to Lisa Tener, an amazing book writing coach, who helped me clarify my vision and provided some invaluable tips, helping me take a decades-long, off-and-on project to near completion in a few months.

I honor Ann Gila and the late John Firman. They changed my life. Their empathy, devotion and integrity was truly inspiring. They embodied psychosynthesis.

Deep bow to Janet Stone. The teachings that flow through her inspire me profoundly on this path. I feel safe within the sangha. And to Jody Greene for showing up as a friend and yoga mentor who guided me to find the time for writing as part of daily yoga/spiritual practice, and reminded me that my innermost heart was devoted to my family and this was to be valued.

And yes, this innermost heart honors my teachers called children: Noah, Bladewolf, Zuri and Tyre. Our love and family support is nourishing and deep, and you help me keep it real, again and again. And "stepchildren" along the path: Molly, Dan, Georgia, Nick, Simon, Vanessa, Erica, Elisa, Shantelle, Liz, Angie. You are all in my heart.

Love and appreciation to many friends, colleagues and supporters who assisted me in various ways throughout the years, including: Jessica Albon, Lauren & Rick Allen, Linda Basso, Mari Biehn, Greg Bogart, Paul Bogle, Chris Brennan, Molly Young Brown, Joan Brozovich, David Chitara, Jan Clausen, Ingrid Coffin, Cathy Coleman, Michelle Cordero, Jean DeFries & June Presley, Monica Dimino, Eve & Michael Ellingson, Destiny Eurkus, Maurice Fernandez, Alexandra Folts, Ana Forrest, Michele Guilbault, Holly Holmes-Meredith, Halfdan Hussey, Johanna Inglis, Jacqueline Janes, Alexandra Karacostas, Brad Kochunas, Klaus Lange, Aviva Levine, Kiki Kristen Lovelace, Chris McRae, Colleen Millen, Robyn Pope, Vicki Robin, Lynda Lou Schartle, Anasuya Sengupta, Mary Simonini, Phoenix & Nelson Simpson, Richard and Victoria Smoot, Gisele Terry, Donna Van Toen, Erika Trice, Judy Tsafrir, Pam Umann, Linea Van Horn, John Welwood, Ginger White, Philip Witkay, Christine Wigren & Scott Hildula, Ian Waisler, Julian Wise, Susan Wooldridge, Kate Zimmer.

Special thanks to the Soul Path Breakthrough course participants. I wrote this material "to" you as my ideal audience. Your responses and actual breakthroughs encouraged me to keep going when I'd hit the inevitable writer's self-doubt. And to all students throughout the years, thank you. I learned from you all. You have helped me integrate these streams of wisdom.

I bow to those who allowed their stories to be revealed in this book. We learn so much from our shared experiences. With most I have changed names and details or created composites; however a couple of courageous souls asked that their real names be used to honor their truth.

I wish to honor my mother, who gave me this body and used her best Virgo/Capricorn skills to make sure I excelled. I know you're still with me, Mom, and the fact I followed my soul path and not the "normal" path now makes sense to you.

Finally, the last acknowledgment usually goes to the one who was there day by day as a partner. To John, you have been my rock in these past years, taking care of the details of our life so that I could focus on this stretch of the path. The humor, comfort, zest and devotion has been awesome. And date nights return . . . until I write the next book.

PREFACE

Soul Path Way uses astrology and inner wisdom to help you discover your true path. Once you understand why you're here, you can live with an authentic sense of purpose and meaning.

Who wouldn't want that? Simple, but often elusive.

We are all drawn to a satisfying, soul-centered life. This quest to understand the meaning of life arises whenever there's a bit of space, a breath on the endless treadmill of life. If not a global or even cosmic meaning, at least some question of "why am I here?" or maybe "is this all there is?" We can get buried in the routine, obligations and expectations and lose track of the thread, though. The endless ups and downs and the meaninglessness of repetitive life tasks can be overwhelming. Relationship karma can bring us to our knees. World events defy logic.

This book offers a respite, a moment in time to connect with yourself and remember the purpose of your life. From that center you can take meaningful steps.

I started writing this material decades ago. In the 1980s I transitioned from the corporate world to offering my gifts as a clairvoyant channel and healer. People asked me to write. I transcribed the channeled teachings from spiritual masters I was working with. I wrote intuitive development training materials, and countless articles on the basics of meditation, manifestation and spiritual development.

As I continued to learn through various paths of study, my client work, and my own unfolding life, I found many spiritual truths I'd originally accepted weren't quite so simple. Lovely sayings like "Follow your heart and the money will follow" are

true-ish, but there's a little disclaimer at the bottom of the angelic proclamation that says *"*the time it takes for the money to
follow is not guaranteed. Your results may vary."* Earth time often
moves like molasses when it comes to manifesting one's vision.
Nothing is simple.

One can learn a lot of astrology from books and lectures,
but until one reads hundreds or thousands of charts with real
humans attached, all of that learning is just theory. Astrological
"cookbooks" are necessary in the learning process, but can be
limiting, dry or often create unnecessary fear.

People work hard on healing and transforming; change is
slow. Feeling stuck is common.

My inner mental wiring is global, integrative. I don't see
things easily in black and white. I couldn't write a single statement without saying "yes, but, on the other hand, this too is true."
For this reason, and because sometimes life takes a lot of time, the
book languished in various computer files, written and rewritten.

Over the years I deepened my expertise in astrology, especially evolutionary astrology—the astrology of consciousness. In
this modern approach to ancient teachings, we look at the deeper reasons for being alive. Destiny is less about prediction and
more about understanding the cycles: what you're here for at the
highest levels, what the pitfalls and challenges may be, and what
the current time cycle asks of you in order to evolve. Karma is
the fruition of past actions, positive, negative and everything in
between. You get to repeat old patterns or break free.

Hypnotherapy certification expanded my metaphysical
toolbox and enhanced my facility with past-life regressions. Yoga
deepened my understanding of how physical practice integrates
with the emotional, mental and spiritual bodies and healed me
personally in ways nothing else had touched.

But it was the integration of psychosynthesis that brought it all
together, and allowed me to work with people in a more powerful,
transformative way. This spiritual psychology teaches that we're

all a busload of inner parts. Some of those parts are working for us and others are saboteurs. Some grandstand and others shrink behind the ivy. The amazing thing to me was that this way of seeing people, seeing life, matched the way Spirit had spoken through me in the thousands of readings I'd done. *"There's a part of you that wants to leave your job because you're bored and in fact, you're almost out the door, looking like a zombie person. The part of you that doesn't want to leave looks like a little old lady knitting booties who feels her co-workers are like family."* Or, *"there's a part of you that looks like a prom queen who wants a stable, traditional relationship, but there's also a punk rock teen who wants freedom at all costs."* From this type of Spirit-guided psychic assessment I would continue on to project outcomes and offer recommendations.

Psychosynthesis-guided "process-work" was a revelation. I could lead people to see in their own intuitive mind screens what I could see psychically and then we could work in a powerful collaborative healing process. Not only were they receiving the deepest levels of truth, they were participating in it. The level of healing and inner shifting was profound. The inner parts naturally related to the planets in the chart; the astrology fueled true transformation. And, not only does Spirit speak using sub-personality language, Spirit always communicates unconditional love and empathy, core values of psychosynthesis.

This work also transformed my own life. I had a rocky road, and we're not talking about ice cream here. Despite decades of therapy and spiritual work, I was still struggling with "karmic patterns," to say it nicely. Like being nice. Not angry, ever—even when a little anger would have been a reasonable emotional response. I have acted out ridiculous relationship karma; situations and choices I can only look back at and shake my head. Throughout life I've experienced addictions ranging from somewhat acceptable to life on the line. The integrated work I present in this book has been tried and tested for a very long time with powerful, long-lasting results, in my life and those I've worked with.

I wanted to write a book that would synthesize all of the tools I've cultivated through the decades, to allow you to receive in book form all the wisdom, information and healing that you might receive in a series of private sessions or workshops with me.

The soul path is the unifying factor for the astrology, intuitive healing, psychosynthesis, and even yogic philosophies. If you're not on your true path, the choices you're making will not be on a solid foundation. Healing modalities won't work as well. Manifestation goals might be completely off course. Discovering and living your soul path is the bottom line.

After all these years I know what works and what doesn't. I understand the nuance of metaphysical manifesting principles. I've helped countless individuals develop their intuition whether they felt they had no talent at all or were already professional psychics. I can offer powerful astrological principles in a simple yet profound, practical way to guide you in finding your path.

You don't have to know anything at all about astrology to gain value from this material. If you read through the book in order and complete the various healing meditations and inner journeys, you will discover why you're here, where you are in your soul path process, and what your next steps are. If you want you can jump around the book, reading only what you're drawn to or ready for, that's okay too. You'll learn a lot. There are many meditations and inner processes offered. You can do them or not, as you wish. To facilitate the ease and pleasure of the meditations, recordings will be available online at www.kaytaylor.com.

Whether you are a novice or an evolved spiritual seeker, this book provides an organized spiritual pathway from wherever you find yourself now into a fuller expression of your soul intention for this lifetime.

May you walk your soul path way with every breath.

—Kay Taylor
Emeryville, April 2016

FOREWORD

Immersing myself in *Soul Path Way* reminded me of a line I used in the final chapter of my own first book, *The Inner Sky*. I had found it in a guide to the local hiking trails: *The map is not the territory.* I hoped that my readers would find the meaning of the metaphor pretty obvious: while astrology offers the finest existential map this benevolent, consciousness-incubating universe has ever provided, we all must still actually walk the life-paths our charts describe. The territory, in a nutshell, is life. We must live it, bravely and consciously. And doing that is what *Soul Path Way* is all about.

I've known Kay Taylor for many years. I know much of her story. And I know she has boldly walked those trails. She has scars to prove it—and the way those scars of hers have healed and turned into wisdom and kindness is an illustration not only of human resilience, but also of the philosophical underpinnings of evolutionary astrology: that we humans are capable of digesting difficult experiences and forging them into gold in the cauldrons of our own psyches. Kay has walked that talk.

Simply reading an astrology book will not accomplish that for you. Memorizing lists of astrological key words won't do it either. Insights alone are not evolution. They can surely *help* our evolution, offering us the map of the territory that confronts us. But ultimately we must do the hard work ourselves: the crying, the surrendering, the loving, and the daring.

Soul Path Way—the title really says it all. Kay speaks eloquently of the soul, of course—but I love that the other two words are "path" and "way." Those are journey words. They are active. They are the words of hikers on the trail of life.

xviii   SOUL PATH WAY

As you read these pages, you will see what I mean. There is theory here, and fine thinking. But above all, *Soul Path Way* is a practical manual for optimizing your evolution. A wise man once said that the only question we ever need to answer is, "Where do I put my foot next?" And Kay answers that one, in spades.

Astrology pervades these pages, but you will quickly find that this is not an ordinary astrology book. The range of topics is broader by far, covering the entire realm of what I would call "mind training." Various forms of meditation, clairvoyance, magic—they are all here, seamlessly integrated with astrology. And, as maps go, that combo platter is far more effective than astrology alone can ever be. Taken alone, astrology trends dangerously toward head games: an endless, futzing fascination with the map itself—a kind of cerebral self-indulgence which functions mainly, I suspect, as a way of avoiding lacing up one's existential hiking shoes.

Kay's aim here is integrative: she ties astrology into a broader, multileveled model of human evolution. Body, mind, and spirit do the dance they are supposed to do. And astrology gracefully finds its right and precious place in the choreographic formula.

A moment ago, I referred to how *Soul Path Way* includes "various forms of meditation, clairvoyance, and magic." That too can be dangerous territory. Reading those words, my imagination is immediately transported to one of those perfumed New Age shops full of pink angels, crystals, and books promising you the happiness that will surely come from visualizing great wealth—wealth that is forever just around the corner. Blessedly, Kay's spiritual maturity shines through here. Her take on spiritual practice is grounded and real. She is "positive," to be sure—but she never slips into the "bliss ninny" illusions of pop spirituality. Throughout these pages, she retains a serious respect for life's darkness and how we must deal with it honestly and humbly. Still, she never loses sight of the radiance at the end of the tunnel. In astrological language, she skillfully weaves together the lofty spirituality of Neptune with the funky, naked psychological passages symbolized by Pluto, Lord of the Underworld.

Kay has learned her evolutionary lessons well and deeply, both as a soul and as an active counseling astrologer in the evolutionary mold.

I always intend the term "evolutionary astrology" broadly and inclusively. I define it as the union of three vectors: contemporary astrology, modern psychology, and ancient metaphysics. I am happy to call anyone an evolutionary astrologer who is doing choice-centered work founded on the notion that unresolved issues from prior lifetimes lead us to having the astrological charts we have—and of course these unresolved issues also manifest as the issues we have in this life as well, those being equivalent statements.

Evolutionary astrology, in this broad sense of the term, probably originated in ancient times. We surely see its fingerprints in the astrology of the Rosicrucians and the Theosophists of a century or more ago. The system couldn't exist without Carl Jung, who was more of an astrologer than most people know. To my knowledge, the term itself was first used explicitly in 1977 by Raymond Merriman in a book he published by that title. I used the term several times myself in *The Inner Sky*, published by Bantam Books in 1984. I do know I was using it in the 1970s before I had published anything of consequence. I didn't actually know about the Merriman book until much later—it was a very limited edition published in the days before the Internet connected us all. For what it is worth, I truly believe the term evolutionary astrology was simply floating around in the collective mind way back in the fertile fermenting casks of the long-lost 1970s. I certainly lay no proprietary claim to it, not any more than I'd lay claim to other then-current terms, such as dudes and chicks, what a bummer, or get your act together.

Jeffrey Wolf Green's first book, *Pluto: the Evolutionary Journey of the Soul,* came out the year after *The Inner Sky*. He used the term Evolutionary Astrology—often capitalized—extensively. He became more publicly identified with the term perhaps

than anyone else. Almost two decades ago, our seminars together and our two joint *Measuring The Night* volumes brought us a
lot of attention. The time was ripe; the community of astrologers
really wanted to bring a dynamic kind of spiritual perspective
back into the system. Our work caught on. Together, we reached
some kind of critical mass. Then Jeff got sick and sort of disappeared, briefly leaving me alone in the spotlight—but by then
our students were blossoming and individuating into teachers,
counselors, and writers in their own right, which brings us to the
present fractal birthing moment in the whole evolutionary astrology movement. Kay's book here is one of its crown jewels.

By the way, I should add that this "big tent" definition of
evolutionary astrology would embrace a lot of contemporary
astrologers who do not use the term to describe themselves.
Within the wide world of what I would call evolutionary astrology there are hundreds, if not thousands, of viewpoints. It's "the
wild west," so to speak. I celebrate that. The situation is vibrant
and human creativity is ramifying. I don't agree with everything
I hear, and I am confident that there are many who disagree with
some of my teaching and writing. Alleluia, amen!

But, to me, every word that Kay writes in *Soul Path Way* has
the unmistakable ring of truth. I am proud to say that she was a
student in my Apprenticeship Program for many years. For me,
that was a great honor. Immediately upon meeting her, I knew I
was in the presence of a deep, ancient soul. When my own life
took a dip a few years ago, I turned to her for counsel without
hesitation. She did not fail me. I'd trust her with my own mother,
so to speak. When we met, I knew I could teach Kay a new way of
understanding astrology. I could impart knowledge of my craft
to her. But I also had a certainty that the seed I sowed would fall
on the fertile ground of her own wisdom.

In *Soul Path Way*, that seed has flowered.

—Steven Forrest

Part One

INTRODUCTION

Swan Vision

Do you remember the story of the Ugly Duckling by Hans Christian Andersen? The little swan was raised by ducks after his egg had accidentally fallen into their nest.

Perhaps you've felt that you fell into the wrong nest?

Or you're trying to get out of one nest and into another and the transition is incredibly slow and challenging?

The baby swan didn't feel that he belonged with the ducks, and he didn't look like everyone else. And they did not accept him. As he grew up, he traveled to many places to look for his true family. Each species he met made fun of him. He felt lonely and sad, wondering about the meaning of his life and if he would ever belong and feel loved. Even when he first saw other swans, he was not yet fully mature, and they didn't recognize him. Finally, he took a risk, entered their pond and was seen and accepted. Only then did he see his reflection in the still water. He realized he was a beautiful swan too.

The little swan didn't do anything to transform or change himself. He simply grew and evolved into his true self. He was then able to perceive himself as beauty. His early experiences with other animals had left him believing they were different—and better—than he was. He thought there was something inherently wrong with him.

We too grow up in a world that doesn't see us clearly, and as a result, we develop a tarnished lens. Through this conditioned, darkened glass we might feel discouragement and self-criticism, or be caught in the endless seeking of perfection and validation by others. We don't know who we are. To be deeply seen and validated is rare.

Our evolutionary turning point is to step fully into swan-self awareness: to see ourselves through the still reflective waters of consciousness, where pure essence, precious and powerful, shines through. And that is where we begin . . .

CHAPTER ONE

(Vegan) Duck Soup

"Before enlightenment: chop wood, carry water.
After enlightenment: chop wood, carry water."
—Zen saying

What's a soul path breakthrough, and why would you need one?

A soul path breakthrough is taking the time to get crystal clear about why you are here. On this earth, at this time. It's about investigating the habits that cause you to make choices to imagine you're safe and secure, when inside you're dissolving into vanilla pudding, folding neatly into a little box you think someone else made for you. Who made the box? You did, of course. Probably with the help of family, bosses, exes, the culture and subcultures you relate to. But at this point, your beliefs, feelings and thoughts are firmly in the role of creating your life.

A breakthrough is an awakening. You might have been working on it for years, or you might have just fallen into reading this book intuitively, with no idea why you're here. Technically, the nature of awakening is instantaneous, like a bright flare of lightning, but often occurs after a fair amount of reflection and turmoil. Many breakthroughs and awakenings arise again and again, like twelve-foot waves cascading on rocky shores. You might wake up and have some sense of who you are and why you're here. Then the next day feels like a blur of appointments and deadlines. You're not even sure you took a breath.

But there's something magical happening right now. We're in a paradigm shift. Despite endless bad news and the planet in a challenging state, our capacity to wake up is expanding.

You might walk down a path, the same path you always take mindlessly, lost in thought, not particularly aware of your surroundings. And yet on this awakened day, for minutes or hours, you see the azure sky as if for the first time, masses of gulls swooping through shimmering trees like a Technicolor Disney movie. So vibrant and utterly blissful you feel that some unprecedented shift is happening.

Next day you spend an hour—just one please God hour—trying to write a page, or even a paragraph, of your soon to be life-changing novel—or maybe just a simple journal entry—while your son throws pureed squash at the wall or the cat throws up a giant hairball on your new black Manduka yoga mat. Back to so-called "reality."

We've all been there. Bliss and contentment followed by frustration and hopelessness, followed by contentment . . . On and on we go, with our limited time taken up cleaning up messes and maintaining a long ago chosen life. Sadly, we don't know how we got to this point nor remember the original intention.

There are several levels of waking up. And just as many reasons why we don't do what we know in our gut is what we're here to do.

At the ultimate level of awakening you could completely wake up, be "enlightened" and know oneness. Exist beyond time. No longer a slave to thoughts, you completely move beyond the framework of human condition and the ego/mind. Sounds amazing, doesn't it?

What you might wish for is to experience moments of peace, contentment and an occasional serving of bliss, all the while knowing you are oneness of galaxies and dimensions and you are actually everyone and everything. To have this perspective is amazing for five minutes or even five seconds. Each time you realize and embrace the truth you are Spirit having a human experience (and your thoughts and opinions are some kind of craziness that goes with being human), you're in a Very Good Place.

At a simple level, can you feel you are on your path, finding the Tai Chi-like balance of holding intention and also letting life be messy and real? If you give yourself time and space to reflect, you can find the balance. You can hear the inner signals. Calling.

Calling is a directional signal on the path...

Calling is when you feel clearly drawn to something without any objectively good or sane reason. Your heart feels open. You feel excited. You just want to do "it » from a place that's so deep inside of you it feels like every cell of your body is screaming. (This is not to be confused with lust, or the desire for an extra-large latte. Or even better drugs.) There is a qualitative difference between a soul-centered Calling and human-style cravings. Learning that difference takes some of us a few extra years. And a lot of meetings.

A true Calling feels important. When you feel a Call there is often a subsequent mental battle resisting it:

"You don't need to do that. That's ridiculous!"

"You can't afford to do that!"

"What will everyone think?!"

"It's just not practical."

Your thoughts will create an astonishing number of reasons why you should *not, absolutely not,* take the risk. If your mind is not thoroughly convincing there will probably be a few helpful people who will be super happy to tell you why your idea is ridiculous. From your besties to random strangers you'll hear:

"It takes at least five years to get a business going!"

"You're too old to start that now; that's a young person's game."

"You don't have a dancer's body."

"You should just settle down with that nice guy with the good job."

With all of this confusing mental chatter and everyone else weighing in on the matters of *Your Life*, it's easy to allow your dreams and Callings, the voice of Spirit unfailingly speaking truth, to be dimmed and softened. Confused, sidetracked, lost in shoulds, shouldn'ts and uncertainties, the months roll by, the years have disappeared. You are simmering in some kind of murky duck soup. You are a swan but still don't know it.

Right now you could be gliding through a crystalline pond with a bevy of elegant swan friends, but a number of choices have led you to a place where you feel you are not leading an authentic, vibrant life—or at least in every aspect of your life.

Is this picture is too grim, too extreme for you? You know you're a swan, floating in a beautiful pond with amazing swan friends. Yet there's a different pond that calls to you. Is it time to portage over a few crocodile swamps of the mind and get to that more relevant pond?

What does it take to make the transition?

We'll start by identifying soul path through a variety of questions. We will weave some simple yet powerful astrological indicators into the mix. We will look at healing process through the lens of body, mind and spirit, cultivating a strong sense of intuition and reliable, trustworthy inner guidance.

You'll need to look at your fears, the ones you know about and the ones that masquerade as Very Good Reasons. It will help to investigate how your mind works and how your thoughts create your reality. The larger picture of mind where we're all connected creating reality together is an often overlooked wrinkle that deserves focus and finesse. You'll explore negative thoughts and emotional patterns that are intertwined; they sabotage your soul path. This requires digging in and dissolving old habitual energy that's been there for eons. As the healing deepens you create a focused plan that you can revise creatively as new information emerges. Life is always changing.

Through the lessons of this book you will come to understand your soul path in a clear and organized way, with steps to accomplish your most exalted goals. We will practice celebrating the truth that you are perfect as you are. Spirit is perfect oneness with everything. There are no words to describe your true nature. There is nothing to fix or correct or work on.

The nature of human life is that somehow along the path you absorbed layer upon layer of false beliefs and now you're wearing thirty-five pairs of karmic overalls, sixteen fear jackets and a negative self-talk hat. This stuff has to go. Time to get naked.

The real joy of living a life that's on your true soul path is letting go of these accumulated beliefs and feelings of lack, powerlessness and apparent blockages. The true soul path way is to learn to live in the moment. This is no easy task. We talk about it all the time and you've read about it, but what does it actually mean? Can you believe in astrology and live in the moment? Can you love the rich history and traditions of family and culture and still live in the moment? Can you hold a soul-centered intention for your life and release grasping and future-tripping to live in the moment?

Yes!

As you start to unravel conditioning so you can feel you're a powerful, perfect swan, your life begins to flow more easily and effortlessly. You move into a "zone." When you are aligned with your purpose, the items you need, the introductions you seek, the creative sparks that manifest divine purpose . . . everything just shows up, often before you've even thought of it. And when it does, it's usually more amazingly perfect than anything you could have dreamed up from ego-based thoughts and desires.

Once you're aligned with your beautiful swan energy, a clearer vision of Spirit manifested into the dream reality, the deeper possibilities for awakening will emerge. This is where some quiet moments of oneness occur, until you find yourself living more from that perspective, and noticing whenever you fall back into limited thinking and ego-mind reality. At the deepest level of truth, you know you are not only the swan but all swans. You are the pond, the trees, and even the ducks.

As you wake up to a greater landscape of meaning and purpose, you find soul purpose is not a singular (nor necessarily a worldly accomplishment) goal as we often imagine in our goal-driven cultures. There are many goals . . . and no goal at all.

Our quest is layered and nuanced.

The objective is to remember and open to innate perfection without fixation.

Each soul is absolutely perfect, a pure spirit. It is the part of us that is the God within. (If you don't like the word God, substitute Goddess, Spirit, Energy or even Titanium.) Here, there is no purpose, nothing to do, nothing to create, no goals. When we touch into this essence of who we are, we might feel a deeply content or even blissful state, although it's a trap to imagine we will always feel this way.

The goal of awakening or enlightenment is to uncover this state of being within. Some masters achieve this state and claim to stay there. Most of us will experience this state for moments or perhaps hours. Occasionally a traumatic experience will catapult us into this state of being, but most often we will find it through meditation or spiritual practice and unraveling the thoughts and feelings of endless conditioning. As we begin to live in alignment with pure essence, striving softens, yet soul-centered calling breathes lightly.

We connect in pure "beingness."

Breaking through to live your highest and most imaginative Soul's Path is an exciting adventure.

Let's get ready to flow.

P.S.: Also remember the part about chopping wood and carrying water even after you know you're perfect. There's plenty of ordinary in every magical step of the path.

REFLECTION #1

*You might want to buy a journal or set up
a new journal on your computer.
There will be various journaling suggestions, meditations,
and healing processes throughout this book.*

**1. Meditation #1.1: The Classic Lemon Exercise—
*just to prove you can do it.***

If you're not familiar with guided meditations and have concern about whether you are capable of guided meditation, give this brief visualization a try:

Close your eyes. Imagine you're standing at the door of your own kitchen or any kitchen you would like to imagine. Spend some time looking around, noticing the appliances, the light source, the floor . . . all of the various details. There's a lemon on the counter. You "see" it there in your mind's eye. You walk over to the lemon. There's a knife on the counter. Cut the lemon in half. You might imagine you hear the sound of the knife slicing through the lemon and coming to the countertop. Bring one piece of the lemon to your nose. Smell the lemon. Lick the cut side of the lemon and notice the feel and the taste. Put the lemon piece back on the counter and walk out of the kitchen.

Write down your experience.

The things you "see," "feel," "hear," "touch," or "smell," in this type of meditation can be quite subtle. The inner screen of your mind might register the visual impressions. It varies for different people, and for different meditations. You might see very clearly, and see colors, or it might be subtle and filmy, fleeting and uncertain. You might see these intuitive images in black and white shades, like an X-ray, and see colors occasionally. If this is you, the color may have a stronger meaning when you see it. You can also "ask" internally to see a color when you don't at first, or imagine what the color would be if you could see it. You might be more attuned to the feeling, taste, smell or sounds. Or maybe you can imagine what it would feel like to do this.

The purpose of doing the Lemon Exercise is for you to understand that this type of meditation is dreamlike and not always in vivid Technicolor. The pictures in your mind are subtle and often move quickly. You can't hold onto them. Always trust whatever visions, words or sensations you get, without allowing the inner critic of the mind to minimize your experience. Generally you should trust the first thing you get and not try to analyze while you're in the meditation. After each meditation, write down everything you can remember as soon as possible. This includes sensing images or feelings that felt stubborn or hidden, the things you "might have seen if you could." After the meditation is over, you might make connections based on interpreting the pictures or sensations. You might be surprised to read your journal entries a few days later when the conscious mind has forgotten what happened in that inner process.

2. Meditation #1.2: The Crossroads

Close your eyes. Gently deepen your breath. Imagine you are outside in nature on a path. Perhaps you can see the path beneath your feet or feel the quality of the ground beneath you. Nature unfolds around you with various colors and shapes. Perhaps there are trees or flowers or mountains or some type of water. Take some time to feel this place using all of your senses. Feel the air on your skin. Hear the sounds of nature in the background. You might even be able to smell the scent of nature around you.

This path represents the path you are on **right now in your life.** When you hear this or think of this, something about the path or the environment around you may change. If so there is nothing to be concerned about; just notice if anything has changed. Observe and feel. Perhaps the path will remain exactly the same.

As you continue moving along this path, you come to a fork in the road. One choice, it may be the left, or the right, represents continuing along the path you're on. The other direction, represents new possibilities. Maybe a directional change. Maybe a higher expression of the path you're already on. Breathe deeply and slowly into your belly as you imagine you have a choice here. Feel the emotions that arise. There's a part of you that might be able to observe with a curious yet empathic stance, able to simply be with emotion. The emotion might be fear, trepidation, excitement or happiness, or anything in the entire range of feeling. Where does this emotion live in your body? Be with this feeling, breathing into the part of the body where the feeling seems to be. If you are not able to track your emotions yet, simply breathe into your belly. Let your breath be your focal point, your anchor.

Now look around to see if there is an ally with you ready to go on the journey. This might be an animal or a being that looks like a person or an energy formation of any nature. If one doesn't show up right away, ask for one to arrive.

Feel the energy of this ally. If you have a visual picture, look at it, paying special attention to the eyes, or the center. Feel into your body to know how you feel about this particular ally. If you feel warmth, trust or comfort, allow the sense of the ally to deepen. If you feel discomfort, fear or uncertainty of the true nature of this as an ally, insist that this energy leaves your space and a true ally comes to be with you.

This meditation is to give you a sense of the feeling you now have about the path you're on and perhaps an introduction to a spirit guide or spirit animal.

3. Soul Path Offering

Here are a few daily strategies to enhance the exploration of soul path. We will go into more detail about daily practice later. This will set a sacred container around the Reflections of this book.

a) The Practice of Gratitude: When you wake up in the morning, pause, look out the window, and be grateful for the day and everything about your life, whether you consider it good or bad, easy or hard.

b) Simplify: Look for moments in your day when you tend to multitask and consider if you can possibly begin to uni-task, mindfully doing whatever it is that's in front of you to do. This can be challenging in the beginning because most of us are quite busy and are used to reading or watching a screen while we eat, drinking tea while we wash our face, putting on makeup and reading the newspaper while we drive (*yes, commuters, we see you*).

You might recall your vacations. Most of us easily slow down and uni-task when out of our day-to-day life. We sit and look at the sky. Lie on the bed or by a pool and relax without an agenda.

Give yourself small moments of time to "be" with yourself. This will allow soul path calling and spontaneous moments of inner truth to arise, outside of meditations and specific processes.

c) Altar: Consider creating an altar specifically for the experience of the Soul Path Way. As you engage with this work, you will receive various gifts, signs and signals from Spirit. You can place any relevant talisman, totem or reminder on your altar: a figurine, a picture or a leaf—whatever has unique symbolic meaning to you.

d) Daily Choices: Pay attention to your daily choices. How do you spend your time? Do this as if you are an ET who has landed invisibly and is watching your life. Be curious but not judgmental. Try not to think (yet) about changing things, although ideas will probably arise. *Observe your life just as things are.* Notice your feelings and thoughts about your life as it is.

CHAPTER TWO

Heart Clues

"Why do you think the thoughts you think?
Why do you have the life you have?"
—Voice of Spirit, asking me this question
. . . again and again

In *The Soul's Code*, James Hillman talks about the "acorn the-ory." He says "each person bears a uniqueness that asks to be lived and that is already present before it can be lived." He shares examples of children whose unique qualities were exactly what they needed to accomplish their life calling as adults.

His book questions the tendency of the psychological com-munity to pathologize and treat childhood personality traits that are exactly what the adult will need to accomplish their life mission—the introverted child who grows up to be a famous re-searcher, spending many hours in the lab alone; the challenging, active young boy who becomes a skilled race car driver.

Parents and society often make assumptions about what "normal" is and try to steer a child to display some perfect middle-of-the-road personality traits they imagine will guarantee a safe and good life. It's not that they're trying to harm the child; on the contrary, they imagine they're helping.

As children we absorb these messages, direct and subtle. They become part of our thought patterns. We are encouraged to be different from our true nature, to choose safety and conformity over our natural inclinations that are actually aligned with soul path. Sometimes we choose a non-authentic self-image in many areas of life. Or we may express ourselves authentically in certain arenas and not in others, thus seeming okay when we're actually just getting by, feeling like impostors in our own lives.

As you evaluate your life's mission, the challenging task will be to perceive each area of your current life from the perspective of higher calling. The entry key is to listen for heart clues.

Initially, you might hear judgmental or imprinted conforming thoughts and beliefs. These restrictive inner voices come from your inner parts who want to maintain the party line. They tend to drown out tender heart clues. These inner parts each have their distinct personalities—their own feelings and thoughts that make up our sense of who we are and how others see us. Inner parts often make our choices and even cause the "reality" that shows up. They are not bad, and we're not going to get rid of them, but for now we'll simply watch them and note their repetitive messages.

You may feel this microanalysis of daily life is not as important as the accomplishment of the grander destiny or overall soul path. That is true. Many of the details of daily life are not a big deal to the truth of who we are. And yet, how much time, thought and energy do we give to these mundane issues? The life we create, often through unconscious patterns and thoughts, gives us the feeling we are trapped in ways we actually aren't trapped at all.

18

Your daily life either supports your higher path or detracts from it

It is relevant and perhaps critical to devote contemplation time to accurately and objectively assess your life from the position of the heart center, to discover how thoughts are creating your reality.

So, why *do* you think what you think? When you wake up in the morning and decide to do anything—change jobs, break up, wash the car, color your hair, go to yoga, not go to yoga—who is deciding and why?

This is critical to know. Each moment holds a choice to be engaged with the deeper levels of who you are—or not.

The millions of decisions you've made over time flow together to create a "life." You're in it. You do it every day, accomplishing the tasks that are expected of you to keep it all together. It seems that you have some latitude to make different choices, but at this "now" moment you can see that you've invested a lot of life force into particular choices you made a very long time ago. As we age, the tunnel of choice narrows—or seems to. More accurately, the parts of you that are in charge of choosing decide some choices are reasonable and others aren't.

You might wonder if Spirit actually cares about the mundane areas of life. Many religions and spiritual belief systems send the message that it is more holy to let go of worldly life completely, or as much as possible. Would it be "more spiritual" simply to disengage from your job, or relationship, or the problem of what is the best grain-free cat food to buy?

Later we will explore these lofty spiritual questions in more depth. However, right now you are living your human life. Even if you awaken fully there are human issues and choices to make. You have a body, for some reason, even if you can touch into the place where none of it matters so much. Assessing to what extent life mirrors your soul—checking to see if the growing tree of You is the embodiment of the acorn of your soul in all areas of life—will be the starting point.

When you examine the current reality of what you have created, you can see and feel what has been created from deeper calling and soul path intention, and what has been created based on limiting beliefs. When you see this clearly, you have an opportunity to "change your mind." As you release what has been created from automatic thoughts and choices, and choose from a more authentic heart vision, space is created to open to the deeper nature of your being.

What are your goals as you think about them right now? You can probably think of some of the goals you set for your New Year's resolutions, your birthday wishes, New Moon and Full Moon ceremonies, eclipses . . . Our ego/minds love to set goals. Usually within a few months, old habit patterns kick in, the intentions drift, and we end up setting the same goals next time.

As you ensure goals are soul-centered, exploring the karmic imprints that create habitual patterns, and offering healing to inner parts, you can be set free from this hamster-wheel pattern of setting goals and then being disappointed when the same experiences repeat again and again.

It's perfectly possible to manifest the wrong goal,
based on desires that aren't
truly in alignment with your soul's purpose.

One reason we often tire of goal setting is because they are the wrong goals. As John Lennon said, "life is what happens to us while we are making other plans." A conscious intention will be more rewarding than mentally chosen goals.

Soul path can be understood through several lenses. We'll explore two in the next reflections.

One is to look at childhood interests and talents. These natural gifts are often pure and clear until you are channeled away from them. Perhaps the family "voices of reason" convince you that your aspirations were not practical. Maybe the family couldn't afford the lessons. Maybe the intense personality needed to accomplish your goals was "just too much"— annoying when expressed through the body of a small child. You accommodated the messages and toned yourself down. Now you're slightly depressed, energy held in a nice tidy ball, and working in a job that suits a compliant personality. The talents and gifts, obvious in childhood, are critical clues to your path. Be aware these gifts often come so naturally to you that you might overlook them.

The other strong indicator of path is to reflect on the experience of your heart. You can remember the experiences you have had throughout your life where your heart opened wide and you could feel your soul singing. These are significant moments when you are aligned with some aspect of your true nature and your highest destiny. You can also think about different aspects of your current life and feel right now whether you feel heart opening or tightening in your belly. The mind cannot distinguish time, and responds with feeling to our thoughts (more on that later). Taking the time to ponder one aspect of life at a time, slowly with breath to allow feelings to register in the body, will provide relevant data.

One caveat. Things that begin with a big heart-swell of positive energy don't always "turn out." Turning out is a concept we have related to our innate desire to have life be "good" and not "bad." Soul path is not about having a good path, or an easy time, although that may be part of the benefit. Path is not always easy, but when we're on our path we are generally enthusiastic about it. Even when it's challenging there's usually something about it that feels good, or at least "right," to us. As we understand this truth of soul path choice, we can let go of judgment about what we've tried that didn't last or have the desired long-term effect. We can forgive ourselves for being human and making choices from our best collection of inner resources.

Let's get detailed.

REFLECTION #2

1. Meditation #2.1: Life Scan for Soul Path Memories
(Note: for this or any other meditation, if what you see or feel is "too much" and you begin to feel anxious or overly upset, you can come right out and open your eyes and be back in current reality.)

Place your body in a comfortable position. Allow your breath to deepen and soften naturally. Take some time to relax with the breath and when you are ready you can begin a life scan to bring to mind key memories relating to your Soul Path for this life. They can include people who influenced you whom you might almost have forgotten, or key moments of realization. This life scan is intuitive and light, like a soft breeze blowing over and around the windows of your life. The part of you that is magical takes this journey, traveling back to the beginning of your life. From here you can touch into different scenes, allowing the part of you that travels to observe key and pivotal moments in your life where you had a sense of who you are or what you are here for. This may be as simple as moments when you said what you wanted to be when you grew up, talents you exhibited, things you were excited to learn, tasks you loved or talents that came very easily to you.

After a few minutes of allowing soul path memories to arise, write in your journal what you remember.

2. Journal Reflection
1. List three to five of the happiest or most enlivened moments in your life, times when you felt alive and heart-centered, with a sense of connection

to yourself. Write as much or as little as you wish about these memories, noting feelings as well as event details.

2. List and write about your moments of greatest accomplishment.

3. Imagine your ideal life. What would you do with your life if money wasn't an issue and you could release anything you consider to be an obligation or responsibility (knowing everything would be taken care of)?

4. What are your favorite relationship memories? (This can include animals, creativity and nature as energies with which you've had a relationship).

CHAPTER THREE
Twelve Life Foundations

"Houses are the medium through which
the earth and the skies connect."
—Maurice Fernandez

The twelve areas of life we'll explore here correspond to the twelve houses of the astrology chart. Each house represents a part of your psyche, the nature of your inner wiring that was part of you at the moment of birth. The houses also represent aspects of physical life, which have manifested throughout your life from these patterns and continuous experiences, thoughts and beliefs. The sign at the beginning of each house tells us about the quality or flavor of that part of your nature, and planets in the houses and their connections to each other gives even more information about you.

Yet here we're going to simplify. Even if you know your astrology chart and the signs and planets you have associated with each house, keep your mind open. Don't think about what you've read or been told about this area of your life. Instead, as you read through each description, close your eyes and feel energy sensations in your body. Tune into what lights up your heart, so that your felt body/energy sense is open and expanded. Note what causes a sensation of feeling closed, tight, not enough, or just uncomfortable.

This reflection will help you explore areas where you can open to a more soul-centered experience of life.

#1 - IMAGE

Image includes the way you look physically and the image you present to the world. It is your persona or the mask you show to people you don't know well and the organic way people perceive you at an initial or surface level.

Are you comfortable in your own skin?

Do you like your clothes, your hair, your smile?

Is your physical body pleasing to you?

When you walk into a room what image do you want to project?

Do people see your essence sparkling through or do you feel hidden and careful? Perhaps your image might be deliberate and cultivated or maybe it has culminated from a series of choices you've made based on direct and subtle feedback over decades. This may be one of the hardest sections of life to be soul-centered and authentic about because we receive such a heavy onslaught of imprinting about our looks and image in this culture. So listen from a compassionate heart to your feelings about your image.

#2 - MONEY

Are you comfortable financially? Research shows most people feel they would be content financially if they had 10 percent more than what they earn and this holds true at all levels of income. Many feel they have *almost* enough, and "enough" is an illusive goal, always in the future.

Do you have enough money to feel safe and secure?

This is a personal feeling and does not have to be definitely connected to realistic numbers. In the field of money, you can contemplate the skills and talents you have available to make money or if there are new skills or a path of study you're drawn to now.

#3 - MIND

The mind includes our habitual thought patterns and the way we communicate. Does your mind run rampant, thinking constantly, the classic monkey mind?

If you've been working with meditation for a while, has your mind calmed down?

On a scale of 1 to 10 would you say your mind is peaceful (10) or subject to endless thinking you can't control (1)?

You might also look at whether you have a natural tendency toward negative thoughts, self-criticism or any other habitual types of thoughts.

#4 - HOME

Home is the foundation of life. This is the physical space where you live and the family you have around you. Family can be the birth family you were born into and/or the sense of family you've created for yourself. Family doesn't have to be traditional in any way. Family is made up of the people and animals you love who give you a sense of belonging.

Consider if your home is too big, too small, or just right, like Goldilocks' porridge.

Do you love the decor of your home?

Are you comfortable in the neighborhood? Are you surrounded by people who feel like tribe?

Where you live might relate to where you work. A beautiful home with a two-hour commute could be an energetic drain. If you commute or travel, is this working for you?

Do you feel supported by the people and animals you call your family? Do you feel love and devotion to family in a way that feels good to your heart?

#5 - JOY

In the astrology chart, the 5th house relates to children, romance, playfulness and pleasure, gambling and speculation. I believe this area should now include pets in the way many of us treat our pets like furry little children. Fundamentally this is the area of the life that boils down to JOY.

What is your relationship to joy?

Do you have enough playfulness and lightness in your life?

What are your creative outlets?

If you have children or pets, are they fulfilling or do you need more support in this area? Perhaps children can bring this light to our lives, but often they can be hard work and a deep sense of responsibility and duty.

There are many possibilities in area #5. What's working and what would you like more or less of?

#6 - HEALTH

Ah, health. The foundation of New Year's resolutions. There are endless theories and beliefs in and out of vogue and yet each of us is individual in our needs. As you ponder your health, listen to the messages of your body.

What's working?

What isn't working?

Health is a daily practice of the nutritional support that's right for you, stress relief, exercise and support from healing professionals. We'll delve more deeply into health in the body chapter, but for now, simply assess your health as it is now.

#7 - RELATIONSHIPS

Relationship includes any committed, bonded relationship you might have: partner, long-term friends or business partners. These are relationships that have a basis in equality and trust, relationships that are worth working on.

Which committed relationships are working?

Which ones aren't?

Which categories of relationship would you like to expand or contract? (As in you'd like more close friends, or you have too many husbands . . .)

#8 - INTIMACY

Deeper than just a marriage or partnership, the 8th house relates to a sense of intimacy, real closeness and bonded trust. Not every life includes another person you can feel this with, so another level of this area is a sense of knowing yourself deeply within.

If you have an intimate partner, do you have the level of intimacy you would like?

Have your explored your psychological depths and touched into your shadow?   Without a fearless journey to our interior spaces we cannot fully experience the blissful realms and higher states of joy.

Bottom line: do you know and trust yourself? When you do, you're ready for the intimacy you crave with another being, if that's your wish.

#9 - BELIEFS

Beliefs, philosophy and the exploration of higher levels of wisdom are the material of the 9th house.

Do you give yourself opportunities to expand your mind through reading, studies or travel?

Do you have a sense of meaning in your life?

Are you living life based on your authentic sense of truth?

#10 - CAREER

At the highest level of career, you are engaged in a work-type activity that feels aligned with your authentic self, maybe even a soul calling. It doesn't have to be a job, but it might be. It can be creative or philanthropic ... your gift to the world, and ultimately what you are known for.

Do you love your work?

Do you feel your work is aligned with soul calling?

What would you love to expand in your work?

What would you love to let go of?

#11 - TRIBE

Tribe is the community of friends with whom you share interests. You might not even know them well. They might be your Facebook friends, or fellow members of various organizations you're interested in. Whatever beliefs or philosophies you are aligned with, there's a group of people in the world who share your vision.

Do you feel supported by a compatible tribe, who might not be close, committed friends (7th house), but rather give you a general feeling of belonging?

If not, would you like more tribal connections?

#12 - SPIRITUALITY

This is spirituality beyond the doctrine of a religion. It is your personal connection to a sense of oneness with all. True spiritual connection sometimes comes unexpectedly during very intense experiences — a moment of bliss or even at a point of trauma. Many people feel a spiritual connection when in nature. Spirituality can be cultivated through meditation, yoga, tai chi and other mindful arts. Breathe into your heart and allow yourself to know if your spiritual needs are filled or if there is a desire to seek more or deeper transcendent experiences.

Do you experience feelings of connection to oneness?

Would you like to?

Do you have a meditation or other spiritual practice that's fulfilling?

Do you spend enough time in nature?

Do you feel supported by the Universe, God, Spirit or guides, however you imagine a higher power to be?

REFLECTION #3

1. Journal Reflection: Reflect on each of the twelve areas of life. Write your thoughts, feelings and physical sensations in your journal.

Part Two

THE ASTROLOGY
OF SOUL PATH

CHAPTER FOUR

The Evolutionary Story

"Good Karma drags us back as relentlessly as bad..."
—Annie Besant

The Nodes of the Moon are an aspect of astrology that are relatively easy to calculate and understand. They are the cornerstone of understanding soul purpose.

There are only twelve basic possibilities. The South Node represents your karmic past and the North Node represents the direction of soul centered growth. We're coming from South and heading North, although it's not a straightforward journey, as you'll soon see (and have undoubtedly experienced already).

Astronomically, the Nodes are calculated from the crossing points of the path of the Moon with the apparent path of the Sun. Energetically, I think of this as the Nodes reflecting the powerful force of the Sun infused into the emotional habits of the Moon. Sun is power and choice; Moon is feeling and memory.

The South Node indicates the emotional habit patterns you were born with as well as the talents and gifts you have to give easily and naturally. If you believe in past lives you can think of the South Node representing lifetimes of achievement and also grinding repetition. If you aren't so sure reincarnation exists, it doesn't matter. You can simply think of this as your natural talents, abilities and aptitudes. You see it in little children all the time. The six-year-old natural caretaker. The two-year-old who is clearly an artist; every wall a canvas. It's clear if you've spent any time with very small children that we are born with distinct personalities and talents. Every planet in our chart and its relationship to the others paints a picture of our life and life experiences. The Nodes are like the core essence within and around the personality traits, the inner soul wiring that underlies the reason for who you are in this life and how you express your natural gifts and challenges.

The South Node represents your karma. Karma is simply defined as actions and reactions, what we have thought, said or acted out, and how that affects us now. It is neither good nor bad. It is simply the energetic scorecard of life. The South Node represents qualities and gifts you have developed in prior lives and the kind of person you were—a kindly king or a vicious thief, although most of us were most often living simple lives trying to survive and be the best persons we could possibly be under challenging circumstances. Kind of like right now. The South Node also reflects the tendency to get stuck in repetitive habit patterns. We all have them. You know, the thing you keep doing again and again and wonder why it's so hard to stop. Acting rational when you want to play. Taking care of people when you wish you could just be more self-centered like your sister, who has no trouble doing exactly what *she* wants to do. We humans are creatures of habit, comfort and repetition.

The South Node also represents your greatest gifts you can offer the world. It's not particularly growthful for you to keep doing the same thing over and over, but other people can benefit from your expertise.

When first introduced to evolutionary astrology it's easy to focus on the North Node as if it's a direct line journey from South to North. But you will notice, in your own life, and the lives of those around you, that this is distinctly not the case. We are stuck in South. We venture North. We meander around with a little of each. Every choice in life often comes back to the balancing of these two powerful polarities in our psyche. We have gifts in the qualities of the South to give to others and also to integrate into the new direction of north node manifestation.

The North Node is always the sign exactly opposite the South Node. It holds the energy we must manifest and radiate in order to feel full, accomplished and on target. Initially the North Node feels impossibly hard to understand, like total rocket science. To manifest these qualities into real life will take time and conscious choice. Yet knowing more about what the goal is makes it easier to take little bites, like medicine, drawing the healing quality of growth and evolution into reality.

Imagine if you were the best chef in a city, known for your creative recipes and ability to create and run a successful restaurant. Yes, you could keep doing this for your whole life and everyone around you would benefit, but after a while you'd feel bored and stuck, wondering if this is truly all there is to life. Perhaps the magic of success would start to wane as the universe nudges you toward growth. Maybe you yearn to study some type of medicine, something you know nothing about, but gives your heart a thrill. This would be like the North Node. The thing you know virtually nothing about, but you're excited about it. The idea that doesn't look practical at all, when you have a nice, safe secure role in the South Node. There's a good chance if you learn more about it, there's a way it can be integrated into the South Node talents and abilities. Now you have both the thing that is comfortable and easily accomplished, combined with a healing challenge. Perhaps the next restaurant is focused on healing foods. Or you actually become a doctor, and head up a hospital that becomes known for the healing food it serves.

The South Node isn't all bad. It's where you've come from. So just like packing all your best equipment before you set out on a journey, you bring your skills and wisdom you've attained in previous incarnations as you venture towards your new goal. However, if you are afraid to strive for the new goal and you just stay at home, doing the same tired routine over and over again, your life will feel stuck and empty. You might experience set-backs, the universal wand of evolutionary growth demanding that you move forward toward your destiny.

Sometimes people jump forward into their North Node goal early in life and find themselves floating on an iceberg, feeling un-prepared, uncomfortable, like a bad actor in a film who doesn't have the full script. The South then looks warm and cozy, the place where they can accomplish easily without trying too hard. There might even be an automatic catapult right back into the lap of habit.

To calculate your South Node and North Node positions, go to the *Table of Nodes* on page 260.

Each nodal position lasts about a year and a half and then changes to the previous sign. If your birthday falls within a few days of a change date from one sign to another, you should ob-tain a computerized chart calculation so you know your actual nodes and even the house they fall into (you can get this through www.kaytaylor.com).

Pay attention to the people in your life who have their Sun signs in the sign of your South or North Node. They are teachers for you. North Node friends light your path and give you hints and clues about your new path, the energies that ultimately will give you a sense of fulfillment and well-being. Watch the way they live their life and if it resonates, try it on a bit.

South Node Sun friends are a different story. You might usu-ally feel immediately drawn to them, totally comfortable, an instant heart connection. Yet with time, you might notice they hold you back a bit. You will fall into your habit patterns as you match energies with them.

In the upcoming section, we will start simply with the energies of the direct route, South to North, beginning with a South Node in Aries. Before you read this, check your South Node position in the *Table of Nodes*, as well as the position of some people you know well. This will help you understand your closest relationships more deeply.

At the end of each segment is a "cookbook" type listing designed to be a quick and easy mapping. *Gifts* are the highest expression of the South Node. *Challenges* are the, well, challenges of the South Node, your shadow side. The *Goal State* finds a balance between the positive qualities of the North and South, not only because this is realistic to balance between qualities that are deeply embedded and those you are learning about, but also because combining the best of what you know with the best of what you're learning is powerful. *Medicine* includes the bite-size pieces of advice you can use to embody more and more of the North Node qualities. And *"When you're off Center"* is my personal idea of how to get balance that is a bit counterintuitive. Many astrologers will focus on the North Node as the goal or medicine for the South Node stuckness. My experience shows that we often jump into North Node territory and feel overwhelmed, adrift without a map. Flying home (to the South Node) and having a taste of familiarity can be grounding, centering and comforting. The "off center" suggestions tell you the healing things you can do that are qualities of the South Node. These things will help you ground into familiarity when you have gone too far from your core. From this stability, you can get back to reaching out for the medicine of the North.

You can see from this there is no "right" answer, and it's not a simple journey from the "bad" South Node to the "good" North Node. You are tasked to elegantly integrate the highest qualities of both the South and North.

Like Sun sign astrology versus a complete chart analysis, if you want to go deeper there are many amazing specifics to explore, such as the house placement of the Nodes, and the various planets that rule, are near or are aspecting the Nodes. The house placement tells you what area of life your soul experience is rooted in and what area of life you are developing. Planets add more detail to who you were or the obstacles you faced. These details could deepen your understanding but are outside the scope of this book.

In this book I offer the Nodes and other aspects of astrology *to fuel your inner study*, to give you powerful clues about your soul path. Reflecting on soul intention from this place of simplicity has its own reward. You can learn a lot about yourself and your sacred soul path from the basic polarity of the North and South Node. When we work from the foundation of simplicity and heal these core issues, we create a firm foundation for exploring the nuance of the whole chart. I offer this to you even if you are well versed in astrology. The more we know, the more likely we are to get caught in the trees, the majestic forest obscured by the scrutiny of the mind.

However, this said, I highly recommend that if you don't know your whole astrology chart and its evolutionary, spiritual meaning, at some point you receive a full astrology consultation from a professional astrologer who works in this way. There is a listing of many reputable Evolutionary Astrologers and those who work with the Nodes and evolutionary consciousness referenced at the end of this book.

Exploring Your Karmic Story Through the Nodes of the Moon

South Node in Aries - North Node in Libra

With a South Node in Aries you have arrived in this life with the karmic imprint of being alone while you faced challenge, danger or a fight of some kind. You are the quintessential warrior, whether it is a physical fighter, intellectual warrior, champion of children, or, just plain combative and feisty out of habit. You have developed great bravery and courage. You start easily and move quickly to tackle any problem or begin a new project. (But you might not want to finish projects.)

You are a natural leader, even if you don't even notice that people are following, captivated by your dynamic inner energies. You probably felt alone as a child, and maybe had to deal with stress beyond your coping skills.

The problem is you don't know how to turn it off. You are in perennial fight and flight mode, looking for danger, wondering if you're safe as you sit in your cubicle typing an email. You're likely to feel that you're in your life by yourself, even when you're surrounded by people or happily partnered.

Your soul goal is to calm down, pure and simple. Anytime you relax and find peace and beauty in everyday life, you are on your path. You are learning about the beautiful energy of Libra: loving, polite, balanced and fair. You need harmonized colors around you, loving partners, a rhythm and flow to your day, and maybe a creative outlet. You might find this boring at first. You're likely to sabotage every calm situation you create, only to create scenes that require your quick skills and warrior mindset.

If you find a loving, peaceful partner, you'll take a job in a company where they fire someone every other day for minimal infractions. If you become an artist, in charge of your flow, comfortable and at ease, you might find romance with a crazy nomad.

With time and persistence, you can find the balance of your vibrant, inner warrior nature with a sense of calming down to find peace, balance and tranquility in an exciting life.

- *Gifts: Courage, bravery, fast reflexes, natural tendency to spearhead projects*

- *Challenges: Constantly in stress mode, combative or paranoid about apparent danger*

- *Goal State: Calm, balanced life and relationships, infused with adventure, physicality and new possibilities*

- *Medicine: Quiet reflection time, soothing colors, stable balanced relationships*

- *When you're off center: Be physically active, take a risk, be spontaneous*

South Node in Taurus - North Node in Scorpio

The South Node in Taurus indicates you have a soul that loves simplicity, ease and the grounding force of the earth. You like things slow and steady. You have a strong need to feel secure. You're prone to like body pleasures: a good meal, a warm snuggle. You love simple comforts and want to believe in the goodness of people, although you've learned to be wary. You might have been a bit naive about what people are capable of, and now you don't know whom to trust.

With the Taurus South Node you have had lifetimes as an indigenous person, a farmer or peasant, living close to the land, bonded with animals and other simple folk. And often what happens in this kind of historical story is that the "bad guys" come along, bringing their diseases, manipulations and trickery. Next thing you know you have train tracks across your land or all of your people are dead. In some way this scenario probably played out when you were young. You just wanted to be smooth and easy and get along; someone couldn't be trusted and you've been betrayed.

Your soul's journey in this life asks you to delve deeply into the psychological and spiritual meaning of life as you begin to understand the powerful energies of your Scorpio North Node. You must understand what motivates people, asking deep and penetrating questions of life. You might have had to deal with manipulative or wounding situations in early life, hanging onto your deep desire to bury your head in a jar of cookies.

It might benefit you to study a spiritual tradition with a long lineage or explore depth psychology. If you don't do this directly, life's experiences are likely to take you to deep places whether you wish to go there or not.

- *Gifts: Stable, sensual, reliable, body-based awareness*

- *Challenges: Slow, stuck, stubborn or latched onto security measures*

- *Goal State: An exploration of depth psychology, sacred sexuality and spirituality with a trustworthy lineage to deepen awareness and capacity to trust, while still maintaining a core level of a secure, stable earthly existence*

- *Medicine: Explore spiritual and psychological things that scare you; develop your intuitive ability to read people so you know whom to trust, and how much*

- *When you're off center: Get outside in the dirt, walk in the forest, get a massage*

South Node in Gemini - North Node in Sagittarius

A Gemini South Node indicates you have developed strong patterns of communication: thinking, speaking, writing. In fact, this may be so strong that your innate curiosity and desire to talk sometimes eclipses a sense of meaningful conversation. Words, ideas, figuring everything out, gossip, superficiality, a fast and busy life . . . you can wear yourself out keeping up with everything your active mind latches onto. On the positive side, your communications are likely to be prolific, and you're a fabulous multitasker. Perhaps all this quick thinking and school accomplishment was a survival level strategy in the early years.

As you get in touch with the Sagittarius North Node goal, ideally you will explore the meaning of life through philosophical or spiritual studies or through travel and adventure that expand your mind.

Both nodal positions highlight information. The difference is that as you deepen in your life goal, you will be less concerned with the quantity of information and more concerned with its quality. Who am I? What is the meaning of life? What is the meaning of everything?

As you get out of the rut of day-to-day details and take sojourns of the planet, sky, soul and higher mind, you will feel your destiny unfolding. You embody the teacher archetype; the world is your classroom.

- *Gifts: Communication skills, curiosity, ability to maneuver*

- *Challenges: Superficiality, lost in the details, monkey mind*

- *Goal state: A rich life of meaning and adventure, connected to nature and wide open spaces, backed up by facts and interesting conversations with people from all countries and all walks of life. You might be a teacher or a world traveler. If life finds you staying close to home identified with a smaller community, the need for expanding the mind through constant learning will be essential.*

- *Medicine: Spacious nature, college and workshops, spiritual studies, world travel*

- *When you're off center: Curl up with a good book or a two hour web surf. Fill your mind with details to satisfy your habit pattern. Have a sparkly conversation about all you know.*

South Node in Cancer - North Node in Capricorn

You have the soul of an earth mother. This will be true whatever your gender identity with the South Node in Cancer. You carry the imprint of the compassionate goddess in your heart, attuned to love, caring, nurturing and emotional support for everyone. Initially, that everyone might be your family of origin, yet as you move forward into life – if you do; some Cancer south node people stay connected to birth family longer than most – you might take care of friends, lovers, work mates, lost animals, your own children, other people's children, houseplants . . . everyone.

You may also feel that those entrusted to take care of you aren't up to the task, and perhaps that's an accurate assessment; they may be neglectful of your emotional needs and not understand your high level of sensitivity. Thus you might come across as emotionally needy or demanding, wanting more than others give, hanging on, fearful and controlling. Your strength is your big heart, and the habit trap is the endless demand of beings who seem to need you. Early imprinting probably included unconscious need from those around you.

As you grow and evolve, you learn to set boundaries and to see that other people will benefit from their own mistakes and the natural boundaries that consequences set for them. This will make your heart ache, because you want everyone to be happy, and you feel deeply other people's sadness, loneliness and pain in your emotional energy field.

Your evolutionary leap takes you out into the big world where you focus on your career or some meaningful work or accomplishment. To do this you'll have to find inner strength to move forward even when you're emotionally overwhelmed. One solution is to create structures in your home life that allow others to take care of everyone for whom and everything for which you thought you were responsible.

- *Gifts: Love, nurturing, healing, caretaking, psychic empathy*

- *Challenges: Neediness of self (even if you hide it well) and taking care of other people's needs to the exclusion of your own accomplishments*

- *Goal State: Loving boundaries, a heart-filled career, structures in your life that allow you freedom to succeed while having a loving, comfortable home base*

- *Medicine: Structure (there's that word again), discipline, mastery, goals*

- *When you're off center: Cook a nice meal for people you love, fix up your home, prune plants, take a bath*

South Node in Leo - North Node in Aquarius

With the energy of the lion as the imprint of your soul's experience, you enter this incarnation with some flair. Most likely you have been in lives where you were special in some way: wealthy, talented, perhaps even a queen or a prince, at least a countess from a distant province. You might display a sense of entitlement from time to time, although often in early life you were not at all encouraged to see yourself as special. You might have spent your childhood imagining how your life would be once you're rich and famous again, watching musicians, actors and leaders of all kinds—and knowing you could have that life. The shadow side of this kind of public life, shining on the center stage, is that you don't get to express your true self. You have developed an image and now you have to keep it up. That is so very tiring. So even though you might come across as self-centered and a bit dramatic, you've lost your sense of true individuality. As a soul, you've been in a position where everybody thinks they know you and they felt like they owned you. But they don't actually know you, they know the mask. They have projected an image onto you, and sometimes, for a while, you've been okay with projecting the image back out.

But not anymore. In this life it is your task to find your unique, authentic expression of your self. Who are you behind the mask of image? Can you be free and alive, perhaps a bit different or rebellious against family and cultural expectations? You're trying to embody the high frequency of Aquarian energy, and there's no roadmap or template for that path. You might find it by devoting some effort to humanitarian or philanthropic causes. You're likely to find many of your soul friends out there in those communities, trying to make things better for the world at large.

As you settle into this path, you might not be so concerned about image and all of its manifestations: your clothes, makeup, car or neighborhood. The position in life you've attained feels irrelevant. You begin to make your choices based on what feels true, real and interesting to you personally, and you are willing to change your mind, your ideas, your life – whenever you want to change. You learn to become a bit more detached emotionally, releasing drama. As you become truly free and individuated you must take care not to replace one image with another, becoming just another cookie-cutter rebel.

This life asks you to use your creativity and special flair to do something meaningful and authentic out in the world, cutting through the images projected on you and humanity. Over and over you're asked to be real. You must guard this life against any rebellious, artistic or conventional mask that hides your real self.

- *Gifts: Creativity, romantic skill, connection to children and playfulness, charisma*

- *Challenges: Finding or creating drama, being overly image-conscious*

- *Goal State: Authentic creative expression, true freedom and independence, balance between romance and individuality, balance between your role in the world and your desire to create art or tend to your children/pets*

- *Medicine: Change it up whenever you can, be spontaneous, don't care about what other people think, see the cultural traps and avoid them intensely, volunteer or take action where your heart calls you to make the world a better place*

- *When you're off center: Sing, dance, hang out with your most fun, creative friends or children, do a creative project*

South Node in Virgo - North Node in Pisces

The path of Virgo karma is the path of service. At a minimum, you have been honing your skills of devotion, perhaps in a spiritual or monastic setting. But even if you were a young monk, it's likely that you were feeding the hungry or polishing the marble floors of the temple. You might have been a servant, a role that defined you and kept you always feeling inferior. Perhaps you were actually a slave. Regardless of the story line theme, your unresolved energetic imprint now carries the blockage of somehow "less than"—in service to others, never good enough, striving for perfection or refusing to even try because deep in your heart is the sense you just can't get it right, life is hard, you will keep working until you drop from exhaustion. Your tendency to analyze everything will drive you and everyone around you crazy. Your anxiety can be overwhelming at times.

In the first part of life, you probably felt you had to deny your needs for others, and now you are likely to attract people (romantic partners, friends, bosses) who mirror this wound—critical, perfectionist people who expect you to follow their rules and do what they want.

As you take in the medicine of the sign of Pisces, you are meant to understand that the Universe is a place of love, compassion and total, 100 percent acceptance of who you are, exactly as you are. You are embraced by God, Goddess, All That Is, the Universe, the majesty of nature. Every way we can name the unnameable oneness, that's what you need to become whole again. You are home. You don't have to do anything. You can just be.

In order to find this state, meditation is perhaps the most important activity you can take up. I would say meditation is good for everyone; for you it's as important as air and water. Any kind of meditation is fine. Hopefully, you will at least sometimes find the place of joy and stillness within and you can soften the harsh inner critic voices that tell you you're not doing it right. *If you're doing it, it's right.* It's good enough. Just breathe. Sit in the sand, breathe in soft ocean breezes (real or imaginary), watch the waves. Simply breathe in alignment with the slow steady rhythm of nature. That's a perfect meditation for you. Or breathe slowly while gently focusing on a candle flame. Beautiful music playing softly in the background is another good Pisces meditation. Yoga will also provide a good meditative experience for you.

You can also use more earthly Piscean activities to relax your nervous system and fill you up. Watch inspirational films, dive deep into a good fantasy book, or daydream and rest in a cozy bed. Bliss is the antidote to your soul-level weariness.

Developing your creativity will also be fantastically healing for you. Your Virgo might be very critical of your masterpieces, so initial creative projects are best abstract painting or serviceable items. As you give yourself free creative expression, you'll learn to enjoy the feeling of creativity rather than critique the end result.

Be careful not to jump too deeply into the Pisces trap of escapism or addiction; the spiritual path ultimately will be your most fulfilling destiny.

As you balance Pisces into Virgo, you will blend the Virgo skill set of humble service and devotion with a deep sense of love and surrender, creating a capacity to serve that is both skillful and divine.

- *Gifts: Devotional service, problem-solving skills, genuine humility*

- *Challenges: Self-criticism, guilt, being stuck, anxiety, easily offended*

- *Goal state: Trusting life and the Universe while engaged in meaningful soul-centered work; expressions of transcendent creativity with interesting detail orientation; conscious connection to a spiritual source of inspiration; balance between work and pleasure*

- *Medicine: Meditation, nature, yoga, films, books, art*

- *When you're off center: Tidy up, organize, do something helpful for someone*

South Node in Libra - North Node in Aries

With a Libra soul history, you have been perfecting your relationship skills. You have a finely attuned sense of taste and proprieties, color, balance and design. You easily see what other people need, and often are happy to comply with their needs. You are most likely a people pleaser, without any thought or hesitation—it just seems like the right thing to do. However, you might also be so aligned with the needs of others in your life that you don't take the best care of yourself or meet your own needs. You might not even know what you need or want, or if you do, it seems like it's not as important as what your beloveds need.

You probably began taking care of people in your family when you were small, being the one who tried to make everyone happy, not wanting people to argue. You are a peacemaker and an excellent mediator. That is your strength. However, your habit pattern may be to give yourself up to others and have difficulty making decisions because you see so many sides of every issue. Ultimately, you might feel most everyone you know is selfish and not "seeing" you at all.

To heal and grow, you are asked to develop your Aries nature. You are invited to see the wisdom of self-centered behavior, even though at first it will seem absolutely wrong to you. You need to learn to leap before you look, jumping into a few situations that might be a bit messy but will be adventurous and fun. You can practice saying directly, "I want" and "I need" without finishing the sentence with ". . . but I'm totally open to what you want." As you begin to act with what you feel is kind of bad behavior, selfish and likely to lose the love you hold dear from others, you will be just scratching the surface of an actual balance between self and other.

Find a passion, be yourself, revel in the joy of life, act, be physical, break a sweat, find an adventure. These tasks will open your heart to your evolving nature.

- *Gifts: Relationship skill, attainment to balance, creativity, beauty, graciousness*

- *Challenges: People-pleasing, giving yourself up to others, inability to make choices*

- *Goal state: Relaxed yet action-oriented, finding a balance between living a life that pleases yourself and yet is filled with satisfying, equal relationships; cultivating a sense of aliveness, beauty and harmony with a bit of an edge; developing more and more independence in thought, word and action as life unfolds*

- *Medicine: Strenuous (as your body allows) physical activity, healthy risk taking, putting your needs first, saying no*

- *When you're off center: Buy an outfit or paint a room in soothing coordinating colors; spend time with people you love who can enjoy the sort of kind, caring conversation you appreciate*

South Node in Scorpio - North Node in Taurus

Scorpio is the sign associated with dark or painful experiences from which we transform and through which we gain power and integrity. The South Node in Scorpio indicates you have been through a life or a series of lives that have been hellish in nature. You have endured trauma and wounding and have come out the other side with a possible (well-deserved) mistrust of people and life. You might be suspicious, and your friends might contend that you are negative and tend to see the worst in situations and people, but inside yourself you know you are just being honest about reality. Evil exists. There's no reason to deny what is obvious.

In some of your "resting" lives, in between the lives of struggle, you might have spent time in a monastery or ashram, trying to understand the meaning of life through ancient teachings.

You might wish that life would be different, but you don't generally expect life to be balmy and calm. Early in life you may have felt you needed to manipulate situations and people to be safe, and an attachment to the familiarity of darkness might be present. Scary movies, attraction to sexuality that doesn't fulfill your heart needs, and intense music could be magnetic to the wounding you've brought into this life.

Yet as you move into a healthier expression of Scorpio (and maybe you started out here with an early spiritual direction), you have a natural affinity for soulful yet penetrating themes in life, including religions and spiritual paths that are steeped in tradition and lineage, such as Shamanism, Rosicrucian philosophies or Buddhism. You might have well-developed occult powers or instincts (without even knowing how or why you know) and a connection to the spirit world. Your psychic insights can be right on if they are not tarnished by fear and suspicion. Innately, you have an understanding of what motivates people, and you might be drawn to studying psychology. You're a great person to have in any intense situation. You will not shy away from tough situations. You are not likely to embrace positive thinking or "woo-woo" new age thinking, although it may be a pleasant panacea to contemplate.

To balance this intensity and to bring about evolutionary growth to your soul, like your cousins with the South Node in Aries, you must learn to calm down. Your specific comfort will be found in the pleasures and securities of the physical, the realm of Taurus. You are invited to learn about your physical body and what it needs to function effectively. Massage and sensual pleasures are spiritual pursuits for you. It's ideal if you have a secure home, financial security and easygoing neighbors. Finding and maintaining a stable relationship with a beloved is likely to be a core goal you feel within to be very important. All of your relationships need to be with people who can be tested and trusted.

I recommend that you have a very cozy and comfortable bed, with layers of your favorite fabrics of sheets, blankets and comforters, and at least a few layers of pillowing beneath you. You have been deprived of material comforts, whether you've come from the emergency room, the battlefield, or the ashram. Creating comfort and security will heal your soul.

- *Gifts: Inner strength, power, integrity, penetrating psychic insight, spirit mediumship talents*

- *Challenges: Darkness, negativity, suspicion, manipulation, power games*

- *Goal State: Powerfully calm, secure financially, physically healthy, comfortable*

- *Medicine: That cozy bed, insurance policies, a secure home, delicious food, a personal trainer or an exercise routine you love, just a little boredom*

- *When you're off center: Read a mystery or deep spiritual material, watch an intense film, or have some soul-centered sex.*

South Node in Sagittarius - North Node in Gemini

The intrepid adventurer rides into town on his majestic horse, then dashes out to the next conquest with a flourishing wave. The pirate and his crew of fearless followers explore distant lands. The prophetic preacher rattles the room with his unshakable beliefs. The athletic optimist and nature enthusiast lives with strong convictions.

No matter which Sagittarius theme you've been living in this life or a long ago past, the overall vibe is one of expansion and movement based on your idea of truth, humor, laughter and the Big Picture. You've lived and died based on your firmly held beliefs, and you're now here to heal a lifetime where those beliefs got you into big trouble.

Maybe this deep soul part of you is getting just a bit weary of endless travels and adventures. Or perhaps it's time to simply know that you don't know. There's a part of you that believes you hold the keys to the truth, and that everyone around needs to hear it from you. You can be filled to the brim with a sense of purpose and meaning, unfounded optimism and hope. The crack in the veneer is filled with question marks and perhaps a touch of hopelessness. Life isn't always as big and grandiose as you wish it to be. Sometimes life truly is chop wood, carry water.

You have now come to the point where you need to slow down and get more information before you speak. You're known for blurting out what you're thinking without a sense of the rules of "polite society." And you need people this time around. The lone wolf archetype is losing its glossy sheen.

You are learning about the Gemini quality of communication, which includes pure curiosity and lots of conversation. Not everything has to be deeply meaningful. Eventually you might find joy in a simpler day-to-day life. Your beliefs don't have to be expressed to everyone you meet. It's great to ask questions, read a wide variety of material and gather more data, always considering the many possible ways of looking at an issue besides your immediate sense of what's right and true—though you still may have much vast, meaningful knowledge within.

As you deepen your Gemini dharma path, you will cherish curiosity and amazement, the simple ideas in life will hold an appeal, and mundane tasks like doing the grocery shopping will feel more fulfilling. You might still feel like something's missing at first, wondering why you don't always have a more important role in life. You might have been drawn to higher learning situations early on, as academic life could have been part of your karmic history. Perhaps you are on the speaking circuit or are a tenured professor. Yet, the simple act of having a cup of tea and a friendly discussion with a neighbor provides a bit of healing, and more in alignment with your goals. You can write and teach and help people as you probably have a wealth of knowledge within; just remember it's not as important to know everything as it is to cultivate relationship, conversations, gentle arguments and the open-mindedness that you're in the process of cultivating.

- *Gifts: Powers of persuasion, optimism, hope, speaking and teaching abilities*

- *Challenges: Feeling alone, habitual traveling, religious zealotry, false optimism, dominating conversations*

- *Goal State: Infusion of meaning with everyday events, becoming a balanced communicator, finding a sense of connection to society and the value of partnership*

- *Medicine: Read, listen in conversations, get to know people different from you, spend more time in the cities*

- *When you're off center: Spend time in wide open nature spots, mountains and forests; vast vistas feed your comfort*

South Node in Capricorn - North Node in Cancer

With Capricorn South Node you are born with a history of leadership. Perhaps your leadership role was in business, government or the military, or maybe simply the patriarch of a family. Whatever the environment, it is likely that you rose to the top through discipline and hard work. As a child you probably felt more mature than your friends, and probably even more mature than the adults around you. Intrinsically you know how to succeed in life and you don't expect any breaks. You plan to work hard, and you do work hard, even at play. You are comfortable with enduring challenging situations when you know the outcome you're working towards and even though you might feel totally alone, overworked, discouraged, blocked or even depressed, you will continue on without much complaint if you feel the goal is worthy. You are a natural born leader, and unlike Aries, who simply have people follow because their enthusiasm is contagious, you understand the value of structure and followers, delegation and teamwork helmed by a true leader. You will work hard for a competent leader, yet you will often know how much better you could get the job done. You might be likely to rise quickly in your work of any type, or in corporate situations, sacrificing much of family life to get ahead. Then what? It often feels empty or you don't get the respect you know you deserve. This is because there is no deep payoff or learning for you in the field of accomplishment.

Early or late, you will come to the point where you begin to value and seek deeper expressions of the heart, the dharma path of the North Node in Cancer. You need to soften and relax, to find a place of nurturing and security in the arms of a partner, the soul of a family, and within loving friendly relationships. You will need to begin by self-love. This will probably be challenging for you. Maybe you'll begin by buying a houseplant. If the houseplant lives for a few months you can graduate to a kitten or a puppy. You might want to develop a connection with the nurturing quality of food or allow yourself to cry more often. You have a lot of grief you've held in for lifetimes.

As you open your heart, you can more freely give the gift of your leadership, without believing your success will fulfill you. You will find joy in helping others find their success.

- *Gifts: Discipline, hard work, leadership talent, drive for success and accomplishment*

- *Challenges: Feeling blocked, alone, discouraged or depressed, lacking fulfilling, heart-centered relationships*

- *Goal State: An open heart, warm heart connections within your successful life, love, emotional connectivity*

- *Medicine: Self-care, loving relationships, crying, nurturing/ nourishing food*

- *When you're off center: Take on a small project, make a list, accomplish your day's goals (I know, you've already done that)*

South Node in Aquarius - North Node in Leo

You are your own person at heart, classically marching to your own drummer at least inside yourself, and as you mature often finding yourself at odds with whatever is considered "normal" in your circle. If your parents are hippies, you want to go to Stanford. If your parents are corporate attorneys, you're perched in a tree saving the environment. You come into this incarnation with the karmic imprint of being the one who is different: the rebel, the outcast, the revolutionary. You may have been dissociated at the time of your death, and now carry an interesting objectivity that is rational and intellectually creative, but at times lacking warmth. Given a chance, you are inventive and original. You've probably had a certain level of brilliance and mentally quick creativity since you were young, even if your mind fired too fast to be able to concentrate on required boring elementary school tasks. From original thinkers who manage to move rapidly up the ladder of success, to individuals who find a unique opportunity to be different than whatever the world expects, you can be full of surprises, even to yourself.

The shadow side of your inner wiring is sometimes feeling fundamentally alone and isolated from people, even when technically you're part of the group or tribe. At the same time you may find yourself on a carousel of activities with friends and their needs and choices, while ignoring the subtle calls within to explore your creative, romantic and playful nature. You might associate with many acquaintances, friends, or interesting groups, but something is missing. Rejection and abandonment wounds might cause a habit pattern of cutting and leaving before anticipated rejection plays out again.

Children can help you explore your playful nature. Any kind of creative pursuit, from pure art to theatre or music, can be richly satisfying, once you believe your life would be worthy without absolute focus on your causes and more enlightened callings.

On the rare occasion you let loose and show up on "center stage" there's an inner soul-centered thrill that can't be missed.

You have awakened to certain truths of the value of authentic freedom, and maybe even a sense of awakening to your sense of truth, and you can light the way for others.

As you develop you find joy in romance, playfulness and a bit of drama, developing a more flavorful image and a sense of confidence. Your friends don't have to share your goals; you can simply enjoy each other's company and a good concert or sporting event. It's even okay to begin to feel you are a bit special, even as you know deep inside we are all equal.

The balanced dance of rational detachment and freedom with a greater access to your unique playfulness, creativity and delight in life will be satisfying.

- *Gifts: Brilliance, inventions, objectivity, devotion to causes*

- *Challenges: Rebellion, cutting and running, detachment, dissociation*

- *Goal State: Creative, playful and romantic from a solid intellectual grounding*

- *Medicine: Creativity, music, dance, children, pets*

- *When you're off center: Read something intellectually stimulating, do something spontaneous that appeals to you*

South Node in Pisces - North Node in Virgo

You are born with the soul of the mystic, one who has experienced lifetimes of searching for bliss and transcendence. Those searches might have taken you into the morass of addiction, confusion and delusional searches, and then to the monastery and ashram to find bliss in a more spiritual fashion. Throughout you have opened your mind but perhaps lost a sense of yourself. You arrive in this life with strongly developed intuition or psychic gifts, a sense of compassion and unconditionality and a spiritual inner life that might often be connected to nature and the power of the water element.

A sense of oneness or connection to the cosmos is your natural state. You can even afford to be against religion or spirituality, because true spirituality is such a deeply embedded part of you that you often don't even realize what it is. You probably feel like you were plunked down on this planet without an operating manual. The feeling of being out of place and fundamentally different from most humans can create a sense of self-doubt that's deep in your core.

On a habit pattern side, your oneness with everything and everybody can translate to a loose connection with truth or absolutes. You can easily merge with others and lose your sense of self, finding it difficult to tell the truth as you feel the pain of the other before you even formulate the words in your mind. Feeling confused, foggy, uncertain and disorganized can be part of the pattern when you're not focused. You might fall back into karmic patterns of escapism. Many have a stint of all-out addiction, but most will find themselves lost for periods of life in giving themselves up to relationships, video games, TV, food or other habits. Your immune and nervous systems are highly sensitive; if you don't take very good care of yourself, you can be prone to low energy.

As you become focused, the dharma path asks you to take care of details and use your considerable intuitive and creative talents for a meaningful purpose. Finding a spiritual path and the discipline of meditation can help you achieve focus, but unlike others who need to explore spirituality, you are simply remembering the ancient wisdom you already know. Spirituality could be another escape for you if you don't apply it to spiritual activism. Your role model is Mother Teresa, not the monk sitting on the mountain meditating for years, although meditation and the mountain will help you for a while if you lose your way.

You can be an excellent mentor for others, but first your own life needs to have a bit more crispness. As you explore "what are my talents and gifts?" the next question would be "how can I be of service to others?" Then you'll be on your way to finding balance between these two polarities.

- *Gifts: Psychic ability, mystical nature, natural spiritual awareness, compassion*

- *Challenges: Addictive habits, escapism, confusion, delusion, lack of honesty with self and others*

- *Goal State: Spiritual mentoring, creative accomplishment, organized compassion, intuitive service*

- *Medicine: Get organized, obtain skills, take care of the physical and mundane in life—like paying bills on time*

- *When you're off center: Take time to recharge all alone or in nature; lock the doors, turn off the phone; meditate, paint or putter around; remove psychic cords you've taken on from others*

P.S.: A Note About Reincarnation

Reincarnation comes from the belief that a soul lives throughout eternity, taking various incarnations for the purpose of growth and expansion. This belief has been part of many religions and belief systems, wholly or in part, particularly Hinduism, one of the world's main religions. Buddhists have a less singular concept of the soul, but do believe consciousness takes rebirth. It appears early Christians believed in reincarnation and that the teachings of Jesus were suppressed during the early Roman control of Christianity, especially by the Council of Nicea (325 AD) and ultimately at Justinian's Fifth General Council of the Church (553 AD).

The Gnostic Gospels, early Christian writings that were discovered in 1945 in Egypt, contain many references to reincarnation. The early Christians fled to Egypt because of persecution by the Romans, although ultimately, the Romans integrated Christianity into their own religion and political system. Some scholars interpret a few passages in the Bible to be references to reincarnation, especially the reference to John the Baptist being the reincarnation of Elijah.

One of the objections some have to the concept of reincarnation is that it is counter to the belief in a heaven and being able to be with God after death. There isn't an insoluble dilemma here if we understand an individual soul to be part of Spirit and that Spirit is one with God. Jesus said we had God within us. Some would say God, or whatever word you wish to use to describe Spirit, is within and throughout everything.

Others imagine there were only a limited number of souls at the beginning of the world and the math doesn't make sense. This is very limited, earth-centric thinking. We only need to read what science is discovering about the continual creation of universes to know that new souls can be born endlessly, and also to imagine that earth isn't the only planet where one can take birth.

Some wonder if we ever incarnate into animal form, or from insects and animals to ultimately become a human. Some believe that if we fail in some way in our lifetime we will devolve into an animal or even to an insect or rock form and have to begin the process anew, a rather judgmental view of life.

My belief is that it is not generally beneficial for our evolutionary goals to incarnate back and forth between species and would be rare at this point in our journey to do so. But I wouldn't say it's impossible for a soul to make that choice.

It is not my intention to convince people of the validity of re-incarnation. I assume it to be true because it makes sense to me in a way that nothing else does, and my experience with past life regressions and past life recall (both my own and the scores of people with whom I've worked) validates the concept perfectly well for me.

There are ample scholars making the case for reincarnation from a philosophical or religious view, and others, such as Dr. Ian Stevenson, who wrote "Children Who Remember Previous Lives." Through many documented case histories, he proves re-incarnation based on lives remembered by children, the details of which could be verified. I suspect there will be ways reincar-nation can be proven in the upcoming years.

In the meantime, reincarnation is a theory that either feels intuitively right to you, or you can dismiss it. If you don't believe in reincarnation, it is perfectly possible to work with energy of the Nodes, and understand spiritual concepts of soul path and pur-pose. Instead of imagining the south node representing qualities developed in prior lives, you can accept the South Node of the Moon represents habit patterns and gifts and the North Node represents learning and growth potentials.

While we're contemplating theories of life, it also seems rel-evant to mention that in the truest sense of "reality" that—if there are "past" lives— these lives or stories are concurrent, happen-ing at exactly the same time. This is because our concept of time and history as a linear process is unique to the earthly realm. No longer just a metaphysical theory, scientists now validate time-lessness through the exploration of quantum mechanics. The belief in time is now challenged, and although difficult for most of us to fully grasp, this too will most likely become more deeply understood in the near future.

It has served us to believe in the linear concept of time and space, to imagine that things in the past happened in another time, that we're in the now moment, and some things will happen in the future. This belief is changing now as part of our accelerated growth process, post 2012. Spiritual traditions tell us that all we have is "now." And then "now" again. As we fully accept and work with this truth of the nonexistence of time, our ability to manifest and create instantaneously quickens.

We can still use a system of time to help us organize and structure our lives. Especially as we explore healing processes, we can shift energy in the past, present or future, and the healing extends instantly to all three time dimensions. Like in the movie *Back to the Future*, when we go back in time, even in our minds, we are able to create changes that shift our current experiences and memories.

You are free to make sense of reincarnation or the deep inner wiring of who you are in whatever way works for you. The important part of the message is opening to soul-centered growth and expansion and avoiding or softening old habit patterns.

REFLECTION #4

1. Journal Reflection on the Nodes

First, read the section for your own South Node. There are many different expressions of these qualities, so think of this material as the basis for interior exploration. We change over time. The ways you express the qualities when very young will likely be different through middle and older ages.

Make two lists in your journal, using the written material as a guide. The first list is the **South Node**: your own sense of your gifts and habit patterns. The second list might include the qualities to which you aspire, the lessons you've noticed repeatedly and the challenges you often face. This is most likely related to your **North Node**. Write the key qualities, both positive and negative, with which you feel you're working within the realm of your Nodal structure.

For example, for me, Cancer South Node qualities include being loving and nurturing — but sometimes giving too much or getting lost in household details, like pruning plants or feeling like I need to cook everything from scratch— when tasks that are more aligned with my true soul's path lie languishing on the sidelines.

2. Meditation #4.1: Nodal Integration

Place your body in a comfortable position. Deepen your breath. Relax and soften with each breath. As you continue to breathe with awareness, imagine you're outdoors, in a beautiful, spacious, peaceful location with a gentle river flowing through. A lovely, slightly curved footbridge spans the river. Take some time to allow this picture to deepen, or simply to imagine you are there and what it would feel like to be outside with water and a bridge.

First, invite the part of you that represents your South Node, the karmic experience part of you, to show up and be with you on the same side of the bridge. Invite and allow this part to show up. It might look like a person, maybe even a cartoon figure, or even some type of energy form like a color or shape. Take some time to notice and feel what this part is like, what it thinks about, what it feels and what its core needs are. Spend time with this part with an attitude of curiosity and non-judgment, not trying to change anything.

Now, invite the part of you that represents your North Node, the growthful goal image, to show up and be on the OTHER side of the bridge. Allow this part to show up looking like a person, maybe even a cartoon figure, or some type of energy formation. Take some time to notice and feel what this part is like, what it thinks about, what it feels and what its core needs are. Spend time with this part with an attitude of curiosity and non-judgment, not necessarily trying to change anything.

Notice if the two parts see each other or if they have any interest in the other. Allow one or both of them to cross the bridge if they wish. Notice if the North comes over to the middle or comes all the way to the same side where you and the South are, or if South goes to the middle or over to where the North is. If they do come together somewhere to meet, simply watch what happens. If nothing happens or moves, that's okay too. It might be helpful to call in loving, healing energy to be with both of them, but what may be most healing is for you to simply see each one with a sense of curiosity. Notice what you actually feel for each part.

When you feel finished, draw this whole scene back into your heart, or safe place, and open your eyes when you're ready.

Write in your journal about the experience of the two different parts and their connection or lack of connection with each other. You might intuitively have a sense of why they moved toward each other—or didn't—and you might glean interesting connections about your life experience through this process experience.

CHAPTER FIVE
Pluto

*"When I stand before thee at the day's
end, thou shalt see my scars
and know that I had my wounds and also my healing."*
—Rabindranath Tagore

Pluto in the horoscope represents the capacity for power. It indicates the nature of an old, deep karmic wound that also holds the key to your personal power. In addition it is the marker for your specific generation. Pluto represents the sacred powerful task your generational soul group has taken on—to unlock a particular shadow energy on the planet and then transform that hidden wound into an integral, powerful force for all to utilize. Each new Pluto generation uncovers the hidden shadows in both elegant and distressing ways. Each sign is transformed permanently through the movement of Pluto over the course of many years. Understanding your Pluto sign adds a layer of understanding to your soul path.

Pluto is considered the planet of transformation, power and integrity. Many people focus on, and perhaps fear, the challenging events we might experience in order to get to the transformation part, because there's something very dark, wounding or even evil within the possibilities of Plutonian events. This karmic energy cannot simply be healed and released. It must be transformed into a radically different energy. The transformation process takes time. A Pluto transit, identified as Pluto moving through the sky and making a geometric connection with a planet in your chart, indicates its energy is affecting focal points within your psyche. This can easily take two or three years, plus many more years to integrate all of the inner changes. Each time you experience a Pluto transit to any planet, your original, natal Pluto wakes up a little bit more. When you experience Pluto transits to your natal Pluto, your empowerment potential surges.

The past-life karma of Pluto might include abuse, injury, corruption, psychological wounds—the unbearably hellish experiences we can barely stand to watch in a historical film. These nightmares are generally infused with feelings of shame, powerlessness, rage and fear. We might be in touch with these feelings, but often they are buried deep within. They surprise us when they surface. Current-life experiences that are similar to the karmic wound and hopefully much less intense allow the buried feelings to emerge. For example, if in a prior life you lost your child in a tragic loss and death, in this life you could have an irrational and compulsive fear for your child's safety. Losing sight of her for a moment in the clothing racks at Macy's creates instant soul-searing panic.

In this way, the dark experiences of this life exist to remind us of the past—to manifest the emotional quality of the wound in present time so that our Pluto nature can be transformed and healed this time around. Reactionary feelings will often include a need to control and manipulate people and situations, and understandably so. In this area of life we carry unconscious fear and mistrust. Trying to control life so this devastating pain never happens again makes sense to the ego/mind.

The real accomplishment of Pluto work is to face life with integrity and courage. We must be willing to dig deep within, to the core of our shadow material. This is the heart of psychological, spiritual and even shamanic inner process. We transform the wound into deep unshakable power. We have walked through the fire and survived.

For the purposes of this exercise we will look simply at Pluto in the signs. The house position descriptions are beyond the scope of this writing, but the house provides an even greater degree of detail. If you do know your Pluto house placement, use the house information in the "Twelve Foundations" to get a feel for the area of life in which these karmic planets play out. The house represents the part of your psyche that manifests the energy as well as physical life places or experiences, like your home, or in your relationships or at school.

The sign position of Pluto describes the quality of the wound and the medicine for coming into your power. The sign position of Pluto also explains generational themes. Although not exact, the socially created generational names are close to the dates of Pluto in various signs. You can find your Pluto sign in a more detailed *Table of Pluto* at the end of this book. *The dates here are approximate as Pluto will go back and forth between two signs around the change years. If you're born within days of a change, check your astrology chart to be sure.*

The soul path power of Pluto may offer some hints and whispers to help you in the creation of your mission statement.

Pluto in Cancer 1914-1939 (The Great Generation) Your generation portrays the power of authentic love, healing, family and nurturing while exposing the traps of enmeshment, family abuse, and conditional love.

Pluto in Leo 1939-1957 (Baby Boomers, who were the first Hippies and Yuppies) Your generation portrays the power of creative expression, self-esteem and loyalty while exposing the traps of narcissism, conspicuous consumption, and the shallowness of the dilettante.

Pluto in Virgo 1957-1971 (Generation X) Your generation portrays the power of devotion, quiet service and environmental consciousness while exposing the traps of endless hard work, resentment and denial.

Pluto in Libra 1971-1983 (Generation Y; Hipsters) Your generation portrays the power of equal relationship, collaboration, justice and fairness while exposing the traps of indecisiveness and superficial social niceties.

Pluto in Scorpio 1983-1995 (Generation Y: Millennials) Your generation portrays the power of fear and fearlessness, sexuality in various manifestations, and ruthless honesty while exposing the traps of the plutocracy in governments, hidden agendas and secrets.

Pluto in Sagittarius 1995-2008 (Generation Z: Boomlets, Planetary Teachers) Your generation portrays the power of truth and the search for the meaning of life, while exposing the traps of religious wars, unrelenting and damaging philosophical arguments.

Pluto in Capricorn 2008-2024 (Planetary Leaders) Your generation portrays the power of discipline, mastery and accomplishment while exposing the traps of endless work and achievement of goals that don't actually matter.

Pluto in Aquarius 2023-2044 (Planetary Revolutionaries) Your generation portrays the power of awakening to authentic expression of freedom and spirit while exposing the traps of rebellion, dissociation and detachment.

REFLECTION #5

1. Journal Reflection on Pluto

As you read the Pluto information, reflect on your personal relationship with power and how power, transformation and fear fit into your mission statement and your sense of being able to accomplish your intentions.

CHAPTER SIX
Saturn

"Life is hard and then you die."
—(probably) Saturn

*"If people knew how hard I worked to get my
mastery, it wouldn't seem so wonderful at all."*
—Michelangelo

Saturn represents the part of us that seeks mastery: real, grounded accomplishment in the physical reality. Just as Michelangelo felt there was an angel in the marble he was tasked to set free, there's an exalted part of us we are bringing into reality through discipline and hard work. The nature of this great work is indicated by Saturn.

Your Saturn sign explains the way in which you master and accomplish in the world of form, and also how you feel blocked and discouraged. Saturn tasks often feel karmic or required, and probably are. This is a lesson you've been working on for a while now, and once again you're presented with the opportunity to get past the roadblocks along the way and achieve your goals. Saturn asks you to set realistic objectives and work hard toward them. Through focused determination and discipline you will mature and develop, ultimately leading to a rewarding sense of success. *Ultimately* is the operative word here, because none of us masters our Saturn goals early in life. By definition, no matter how much success you achieve early on, true mastery takes decades.

Reflecting on your Saturn sign, even in this general way, may provide some interesting food for thought as you consider your soul path intentions. It illuminates a significant piece of your karmic puzzle. If you happen to know the house position of your Saturn, you will also know the area of life where you are learning Saturn lessons, but you will probably simply know what area of life Saturn is operating in. Where do you feel you make mistakes over and over? If you're older, where did you accomplish something you're proud of through trial and error?

Saturn lessons are challenging, and people who know anything about the transits of Saturn often tremble at the thought of one. Yet if you look back, you'll see that each time you've been forced to face hard realities, mature and deepen, the work was well worth it in the end.

Saturn changes signs every two and a half years. You can find your Saturn sign position in the table on page 264.

Look at your Saturn sign for keywords to meditate on. Contemplate this sentence with your Saturn keywords:

"In this life and in former lives you have felt blocked from experiencing the highest levels of these Saturn qualities, and will work hard (or have worked hard) in this life to develop and master them fully."

Saturn in Aries: Boldness, bravery, courage, self-reliance and independence

Saturn in Taurus: Smoothness, steadiness, ease, security and comfort

Saturn in Gemini: A talent for communication of all kinds: writing, speaking and teaching

Saturn in Cancer: Love, healing, nurturing, relationship security and nourishing home life

Saturn in Leo: Creative expression, validation, prominence and the feeling of being seen

Saturn in Virgo: Skillfulness, service, the joy of perfectionism, and appropriate devotion

Saturn in Libra: Balance, peace, harmony, clear relationships, artistry

Saturn in Sagittarius: Truth, meaning and exposure to different ideas and cultures

Saturn in Scorpio: Deep unshakable power, depth, intimacy and trust.

Saturn in Capricorn: Excellence, accomplishment, mastery, a "great work"

Saturn in Aquarius: Awakening, authentic freedom, unique expression, and individuation

Saturn in Pisces: Compassion, transcendent creativity, direct spiritual connection, clear intuition

REFLECTION #6

---

1. Journal Reflection on Saturn

As you read the Saturn information, reflect on both the way you might feel blocked or frustrated by the sign quality of your Saturn, and also how the evolved energy of that sign is your ally on your intentional journey to accomplish long-term goals.

CHAPTER SEVEN

Soul Path Mission Statement

"Sankalpa is the subtlest level of intention at the cusp of choiceless awareness and thought."
—Deepak Chopra

Now it's time to write a Mission Statement. This is different from a typical to-do list or a list of "resolutions" that are driven by the ego, because you've been digging deep to uncover the heart and soul of your true nature. This is a soul path mission that is infused with the deeper intention for the whole life, even though you may also have aspects of mission that relate to seemingly worldly goals like relationship, abundance or occupation. The ancient word for this sense of purpose aligned with soul awareness is *Sankalpa*.

Your Mission statement is always in motion. It is never static. It doesn't have to be perfect or forever. Just write whatever you feel is true right now. Often the Karmic Story material and the meditation to integrate the South and North Nodes can be core influences for your understanding of your Mission. The twelve foundational areas of life tend to point out the sub-missions, the thorny unresolved issues or parts of life that aren't smooth or accomplished yet.

When Elena did the meditation to allow the North and South Node inner parts to meet on the bridge, she was surprised by what emerged. She'd been aware of her astrology chart for years, so she thought she understood her disciplined Capricorn South Node and the desire to bring more love and acceptance into her life with her Cancer North Node. Her North Node is placed in the career area; she assumed that developing the Cancer North Node would evolve her teaching work in the world to be softer and more healing.

In her meditation, the South Node showed up looking like a conservative, strong woman, competent and skilled. The North Node was a tall and beautiful being—flowing, light and soft. Not a surprise. Both parts were easily willing to meet in the middle of the bridge and connect. The Cancerian North Node part told her she was actually going to help her deepen her relationship with her boyfriend—that she needed a deep, committed relationship before she could go out more fully into the world, that this too was part of her destiny. Elena could see the driven Capricorn South Node was still all about business and accomplishment, focusing now on loving accomplishment, but accomplishment all the same. The feeling of love and support she received from the North Node image provided a strong inner shift. The two parts weren't working against each other; the North wanted to help with the integration—including the development of intimate partnered relationship.

Going into the details of the chart, this makes sense. Her Moon is aligned with a Cancer North Node and in a square aspect to the Nodes and also connected to planets in the marriage area of the chart, the 7th house. This alerts us to the fact that a deeper level of relationship must be accomplished as a "skipped step" before the ultimate North Node career would manifest fully. It was healing for Elena to be given this very specific information in her meditation. She didn't know this complex level of astrological interpretation. She felt empowered and supported to know an inner part was helping her with the healing and integrative process. She thus released feelings of struggle and hard work from the Capricorn side in an effortless way. Her Mission Statement then wove the goal of love and nurturing into not only her career but also to a goal of conscious, committed relationship. She could take a deep breath and relax. She also knew she'd have to express some loving boundaries (Cancer/Capricorn blend) to find the balance she wished for in her relationship.

Janine was born with a completely different nodal structure: South Node in Leo and North Node in Aquarius. In her first meditation, she saw the South Node as a King. He was perceived as strong by those around him, but inside he felt out of touch. He had kind eyes and a big heart, but he was hidden behind a gold-colored robe and a large crown.

Her Aquarian North Node showed up in the meditation as an Angelina Jolie-type person squatting down among children. The king seemed interested in crossing the bridge to see her but wasn't ready to leave his "kingliness" behind. He watched with curiosity.

This didn't feel like a total "outcome" to Janine, although I would stress there never has to be an outcome in these meditations. The important thing is to feel and see with curiosity and empathy for each part to allow them to unfold naturally over time. Giving them space and attention is the healing power. Checking in on parts from time to time, or doing the meditations more than once, allows the parts to feel more completely seen without a sense of forcing change.

Janine therefore did the meditation a second time a few weeks later. This time the King was wearing casual clothes underneath his robes and was stretching, like he was getting ready to go for a jog. The North Node Aquarian woman was sitting cross-legged with both children and animals all around her. The South Node King noticed that the North Node female saw him in his casual clothes. He took off his crown. He stayed on his side but let the woman see him with the robe open and the crown off. Janine felt he was starting to reveal his authentic self.

Two months later, Janine did the meditation a third time. This time the King took the crown off, let his long hair down, and was ready to go across the bridge. The North Node, in true Aquarian style, was flashing different images of herself, including lying on a lounge chair, smoking a cigarette—the rebel indeed. Janine felt they were both relaxing into themselves and would now begin to work together. The word "Santosha" came to her: contentment with what is. *We'll be working with Santosha and other Yama and Niyama contemplations in Chapter 19.*

As Janine did this work over several months, she gained clarity that her corporate job was no longer of interest to her. She wanted to use her considerable skill at a nonprofit organization or find a completely different career. This wasn't totally new to her; she'd thought of working at nonprofits before. It just didn't seem practical. She now could see how image and an unconscious expectation that she make enough money to live a lavish lifestyle had infused her choices. The life course had been set with choices early on, but with this inner work she could see the karmic pattern. This was painful, but freeing. She now had clarity for her Mission Statement.

REFLECTION #7

1. Journal Reflection: Use your previous journal entries, meditations and contemplation of all of the previous chapters to define the path. Maybe you have some other ways of accessing your inner vision, such as Runes, Tarot cards, or a vivid dream.

Write a Soul Path Mission statement with some sub-missions.

My Soul Path Mission Statement is _____

_____

And my sub-missions include

_____

_____

For example, my current Mission Statement is:

I use my intuitive/spiritual power to bring love, self-acceptance and healing to the world

(South Node Cancer ruled by Moon in Pisces, North Node Capricorn ruled by Saturn in Scorpio)

Sub-missions include:

- *Working with individuals and groups*

- *Supporting my adult children to live their soul paths*

- *Letting other people take care of my home so I can focus on work*

- *Writing books*

Part Three

FOUR PILLARS
OF HEALING

CHAPTER EIGHT

Where do you Start?
Perhaps Where You Are?

"Each of you is perfect the way you are . . . and
you can use a little improvement."
—Shunryu Suzuki

At this point, you have evaluated your life within a framework of soul path based on your felt experience and some powerful astrological indicators. Hopefully you have clarified your intentions into a written Soul Path Mission Statement with some smaller goals as well.

As you gave your life this focused attention, you may have found both troublesome and stuck perspectives and other situations that changed almost without effort. It doesn't take much thought to release minor stuck patterns that you were barely noticing. There can be surprising instantaneous shifts in both the way you perceive reality and how reality shows up to greet you.

In this next segment we continue to fine-tune your soul path intentions and goals. We will explore the framework for the healing process, and deepen your understanding of how transformation occurs.

If you're feeling a bit overwhelmed or haven't had time to do every single reflection or meditation of the previous weeks, that's okay. Take your time and complete what you feel called to do.

How do people transform or awaken? Often it is the experience of pain or intense challenge that draws us to explore new alternatives. There's a shift point where all of our previous coping mechanisms don't work and we can't hold it together anymore. We can't tell ourselves the same stories. It's almost as if we're forced to change. If we think about it, we might wonder who is doing the forcing. What is the inner dynamic that leads us through a cycle of soul-weary unhappiness to a crisis, and then to a shift in perspective that allows us to change instantly— or gives us the strength to do the work to create lasting transformation?

Although an event-based universal push is the most common way to evolve or grow, it doesn't have to be that way. We have choice. If you put your hand on a hot burner two or three times, the next time you see a burner you can choose whether or not you're going to put your hand on it, wondering if it's hot this time. We've all been there. You can even decide you are naturally so inclined to place your hand on hot burners that you become a raw foods vegan and totally avoid kitchens.

Louise Hay's groundbreaking book *You Can Heal Your Life* struck a chord with me when it was published in 1984. This was the exact year I left my corporate job and deepened my healing path.

Louise wrote that in order to change, you didn't have to use her ideas of positive thought. She taught that you could heal using mental (thought or emotions), spiritual or physical techniques, and it didn't matter where you started as long as you ultimately healed on all levels. She also wrote that you could just start with whatever you were drawn to and ultimately you'd naturally be drawn to the other healing techniques.

At that time, I had been in therapy for two years and was very active physically. I had begun to meditate, was reading self-help books, and would soon dive deep into spiritual pursuits. The idea that positive thought was the key to changing one's life was a new and fairly radical idea of the time. Since then a LOT has been written about positive thought and mind manifestation principles; the successful documentary *The Secret* brought these philosophies to a wider audience.

However, back in the 1980s, I found working with these principles on my own and with my very first clients to be mixed. This was new territory, sometimes positive and fruitful, yet often slow and discouraging.

I'll share with you insights I've learned over the years that will help you use all four pillars of healing: mental, emotional, physical and spiritual. With an integrated, full-spectrum approach, you can release whatever is not in complete alignment with your current stated soul path intentions and create new ways of being in the world, drawing power and energy to you.

Your intentions are not static

*Your goals are best held in a field of conscious
relaxation and acceptance.
This is your life and these are your goals.
You get to play with them.*

Now that we are digging into the healing part of the journey, I want to remind you again that you are, in fact, already perfect as you are. As you deepen your breath into the quiet and perfect space of your essence, the healing journey will be not only lighter and more fun, but much more successful.

To paraphrase Louise, it doesn't matter how you start this healing journey. You will be led perfectly from your unique starting point into the other areas. Healing will permeate all of the various aspects of your life.

The pain of divorce might lead to therapy. As you explore the emotional pain, you might realize you wish to take better care of yourself so that you choose more exercise and give yourself the gift of regular massage. As you rest in a nourished body, you might feel good enough to consider deeper spiritual issues or the meaning of life.

It's a whole lot easier and less painful to initiate healing when you hear the early intuitive whispers. These clues are meant to draw you toward more conscious choices rather than waiting for the sledgehammer of event experience to be the wake-up call.

When we ignore the need for healing, it often finds us in creative ways that are not initially as pleasant.

An example of healing brought on by a wake-up call and then morphing from one pillar to the next came from James.

James was a stockbroker in his late fifties who liked a good steak and fine wine. When he was 49 years old, he was in a multi car accident that placed him in physical therapy three times a week for several months. After many sessions, impatient with the slow progress, he asked his physical therapist what he could do on his own to speed his recovery. She suggested Tai Chi. He scoffed at the idea at first, as he wasn't the type to do something like this. Actually, when she mentioned it, he didn't even know what Tai Chi was, but he wanted to be free of pain and trusted his therapist.

Soon he enjoyed the slow, gentle movements of Tai Chi and felt much more flexible; in fact, he began to feel better than he ever had with years of working out with weights. The meditative process relaxed his mind, and, feeling better now mentally and emotionally, he found it easy to eat better. He'd always known he should eat more vegetables and less meat and alcohol but it was a habit of his life and his cohorts.

As he felt better, he simply made better choices. He lost thirty pounds that he had always thought of as having a naturally stocky body type. His Tai Chi friends talked about different books and websites that he'd never heard of. Quietly he began to explore an entirely new direction of thought. He became an assistant Tai Chi teacher, which reminded him that when he was a child he had always imagined he would be a teacher when he grew up. Life had taken an entirely different path.

James quit his job to explore his lifelong dream of teaching.

The car accident, an event that most people would consider a problem, became a major positive turning point in his life.

Can you think of a traumatic or emotionally challenging event in your life that caused you to seek one form of healing? Did it lead to other levels of healing?

In this chapter's Reflections you'll be looking at this question in more depth.

It doesn't matter how you start your healing journey, you just have to take one step—any step. In fact, every step is a healing step when looked at from the perspective of perfection at the core of all of life.

We are already perfect.

We could use a little improvement.

We start where we are.

We often hear the phrase "body, mind, spirit." We will reverse the order, beginning where it all starts: Spirit. From the spark of consciousness and spiritual overview through mental and emotional layers to manifested physicality: Spirit, Mind, Body.

The Four Pillars of Healing

SPIRITUAL HEALING

Spiritual healing includes feeling your connection to Spirit through nature, meditation, prayer or contemplation. You get to understand yourself as part of a vast universe. As you connect with your inner spiritual parts, Spirit guides and allies, you have an opportunity to feel guided, protected and loved. Developing your intuition is part of spiritual healing. Inner guidance, Spirit assistance, signs and magic are all available to guide you on your path. When you (your ego/personal self) are aligned with You (Higher Self), miracles happen.

MIND HEALING

Mind Healing is divided into two components: **emotional healing** and **mental healing.** You'll see that they work together and are often the stumbling block when you attempt to create change via positive thinking. Negative emotional patterns, held strongly by inner parts, often sabotage mental healing. Despite emotional clearing, habitual thoughts can be overpowering.

BODY HEALING

Body healing, or the realm of the physical, is the fourth pillar of healing. Here we will explore physical health and getting comfortable in your own physical skin. You're probably familiar with the phrase "the body is the temple of the soul." It is. Sometimes that temple is dilapidated and needs major renovation and a thorough cleaning.

The body is the physical manifestation of the soul's vibration. Take good care of it to allow mind to be clearer and a more true expression of Spirit.

In this segment we will also talk about taking conscious actions as part of spiritual path. Without this, all the positive thought, emotional clearing and spiritual questing is missing the important quality of intentional action.

SUMMARY

We will assess all four pillars of healing as they are in your life right now. As you deepen your awareness and skill level, you will most likely adjust your healing path so that it is more attuned to the Soul Path Mission and subgoals you have created for yourself.

Every goal you have, whether to create something amazing or to release something that no longer serves you, can be considered in relationship to these four key areas of life.

How will you begin? Whether you are called to deepen your spiritual path, or to heal and release emotion, to understand your mental attitudes and how your thoughts are creating your reality, or to heal the physical body or take positive actions, the next chapters will explore life through each lens.

REFLECTION #8

1. Journal Reflection #1: Continue to consider and fine-tune your Soul Path Mission statement and subgoals. You may find new ideas and synchronicities coming to you now that you have opened up this line of inquiry.

2. Journal Reflection #2: Consider each of the Four Pillars of Healing as they operate in your life right now. Write a paragraph or two in your journal about how you feel about these areas, like taking a "before" photo. We'll take the "after" photo in Chapter 19.

SPIRIT:
What is your current spiritual practice or path?
How do you feel about it?
What would you like to add or subtract?

MIND:
Mental Mind
Do you have habitual thought patterns?
Are you comfortable with your mental ability to manifest?
Do you have moments or stretches of mental quiet?
Emotional Mind
How is your capacity for joy and happiness?
Do you have older emotional material stored or emotions that arise regularly that you reject?
Do you have people (therapists, nurturing, listening friends) with whom you feel safe to explore your emotional terrain?

BODY:

How is your physical care/exercise practice? How comfortable are you in your body?

How do you feel about taking actions in the world that relate to your path? Ready to jump in? Or more like, "You're going to have to drag me out of the closet!"

3. Meditation #8.1: Feeling All Four Pillars

This is a great meditation to align with all four aspects of self. It will get you in the right framework to do the reflection exercise above, and will probably feel grounding and centering to do any time. You can learn to do this in just a few moments whenever you need to center yourself.

Place your body in a comfortable position. Deepen your breath. As you breathe, feel the breath move throughout your entire body, as if you could breathe to the ends of your fingers and toes. Feel the breath soften and relax the belly, with a gentle expansion of your ribs in all four directions.

As you breathe, begin to feel into the physical body, as it is right now. Each breath gently touches into an area, perhaps starting at the head and moving down, or simply allowing the breath to move intuitively into various areas.

How is your physical body feeling right now? Notice the body and any physical sensations, subtle or strong, without necessarily trying to change anything. Simply be with your physical presence, as it is.

Now, feel into your emotional state. How are you actually *feeling* in this moment? What is your mood? Perhaps you notice one strong feeling or maybe there are several different emotions . . . maybe feelings are unclear or nebulous. If you are willing, breathe into each feeling and track where it is living in your body. Is it surface or fleeting? Is it deeper?

Strong or light? Simply be with your emotional state, in this moment, without necessarily trying to change anything.

As you continue to deepen your breath, connect to your mental state, in this moment. Is your mind quiet and soft, or is it active and shifting, busy or anxious? Simply notice the state of your mind. You might feel your mental mind is in your head and breathe some softening breaths to your head, or you might find an aspect of mind in the heart, upper belly area or another area of the body. Perhaps thoughts soften as you breathe softly into your heart space or maybe they resist and become stronger. It is not necessary to struggle with your mind or to try and force anything. Simply notice the mental activity and be with the breath.

Finally, allow your perception to expand to include Spirit—that which is inside you and that which is all around you. As you breathe into this deep quiet core of stillness within, you might feel a sense of presence that holds you, a presence that is always there even when you are not feeling, not listening. Allow your breath to soften into this place.

Feel free to stay as long as you wish. You may go back to explore the physical, mental and emotional feelings again, or feel all four areas at once.

When you are ready, open your eyes.

You may wish to journal about your experience.

CHAPTER NINE
The Spiritual Pillar

"To be in a true and mature relationship
with a spiritual teaching
requires you to apply it, not simply believe in it."
—Adyashanti

One moment you're part of the cosmos, a drop of pure water in the vast ocean of consciousness. In the next moment, you've manifested into the physical dimension, a sense of jumping down the Earth slide into a tiny bundle of flesh called a baby. Yet you're still part of the quiet vastness, a feeling beyond bliss, power and love, but those are the best words in this language that can describe your presence.

It's not like this is a surprise. You've been aware for some time (except there isn't any time where you are) that all the threads are coming together for another adventure in physical form.

You have a big agenda and many small ones. You are all powerful and all knowing. This is going to be great . . .

. . . And then you forget it all.

Soul Purpose: The Wake-Up Game

The spiritual path is a journey of remembering. From small conscious choices like remembering to look at the sky with a moment of gratitude, to deeper commitments of devotional practice, church attendance or weeklong meditation retreats, spiritual healing asks that you find ways to awaken.

Although we use the words "spiritual healing," what we often call "your spirit" doesn't need any healing at all. In fact, it isn't even yours. You are its human manifestation in the field of form, truthfully. It is the many layers of mistaken identity masking spirit that need to be dissolved, melted and released. The path asks us to shed attachment to thought-driven life while still engaging in life actively. You did make that jump down the slide, after all.

A spiritual awareness of life includes understanding and using your intuitive gifts, but intuition is a natural life tool and not a substitute for a spiritual path. We will cultivate an intuitive connection with Higher Self and the spirits who support the journey, because there is a richness in receiving intuitive messages, noticing fascinating synchronicities and learning to see and interpret symbolic imagery.

 . . . *You're feeling alone and uncertain about a decision and a hawk that isn't supposed to be in your state shows up and sits on your balcony, staring right at you. Hawks are messengers. What is the message you're getting?*

 . . . *You're questioning a job offer and a snake slithers up to your car in the city. You blink because you're not sure if it's real or not. If you don't know the symbolic meaning of snake, you might look it up to discover the traditional meaning is transformation and empowerment.*

Life offers preliminary intuitive whispers. If we don't listen and interpret the messages we receive, life events occur to deepen the message.

Any experience that is out of the ordinary, shocking, strange or unexpected, can be a catalyst to help us wake up. Uranus is the planet of awakening, and its connected sign, Aquarius, also indicates where you might be prone to wake-up calls. Its activation in your chart will indicate unexpected experiences designed to shake you out of your sleepy doldrums. It would be great to stay awake and aware, although that doesn't usually happen in a straight line (not very Aquarian, those straight lines). Usually we wake up for a moment and then get sleepy again and then wake up again . . . on and on like an endless alarm clock snooze button . . . until we stay awake more often and asleep much less.

Many spiritual healing stories start with something like, "I just woke up one morning and knew I had to . . . start meditation . . . go to a yoga class . . . find a teacher or mentor . . . go spend some time near the ocean and "find myself."

When you find your true spiritual path it is almost impossible to step off. There's something about it that feels right and feeds your Spirit nature. Life before this path feels empty or hollow. There might be a period of experimentation and discovery where you try different teachers or lineages. Initially your family's beliefs might have had an impact on you, as something you either embraced or rebelled against. The family tradition might have been exactly right for you, or a part of it might still resonate (like going to church at Easter or Christmas). Or, you might have completely rejected your early religious training and gone in a completely different direction.

There is a review of various traditions on the way to one's true path. It's as if you have to check them off the list, remembering perhaps what you knew in a prior life.

. . . *Ah yes, the Jesuits, that still feels resonant. I liked the simplicity of Buddhism, but the Shaman lives were my deepest experiences of awareness . . . Or, I don't trust any of them. Stay away.*

You don't have to believe in God or any particular deity to have a spiritual path. An open mind and the understanding there is something greater that connects us all can be a perfect starting point.

The rigidity and hypocrisy of religious institutions through-out history have left many individuals wary of spirituality. If that's you, remember there is a huge difference between religion and spirituality. Your starting point might be to notice how you feel when you're in nature. A hushed redwood forest or crashing waves at sunset can be as awesome and spirit-infused as a Zen meditation retreat or cathedral.

A spiritual path asks you to cultivate a belief system that res-onates with you and then be with those beliefs with mindfulness and attention. Discipline in following recommended practices may help to deepen spirituality, but rigidity at the expense of in-ner truth may not ultimately work. There's an exquisite balance that requires inner listening.

I remember waking up at 6:30 a.m. on New Year's Day, ex-pecting to do my morning yoga practice and then begin cooking a festive dinner for the family. Instead, I saw that my partner was up and dressed and needed me to take him to the hospital. Thus my practice that morning was to stand at the window, look at the sky and take three deep breaths as I lifted my arms overhead and back to my heart, before heading downstairs to jump into the car. The spiritual practice of the day was to let go of my at-tachment to the plans for the day, to be devoted with a peaceful heart to another's needs, and to stay centered and calm in the face of an emergency. Situations like this ask us to be willing to be with the moment in life as it arises, rather than disagreeing with it and wanting it to be different. Yet it was the inner calm cultivated from years of meditation and yoga that allowed me to be with that moment without struggle, to appreciate the three big breaths, and to do a few yoga poses in the ER while he went off for tests.

Your spiritual path could include prayer, meditation, spiri-tual reading, time alone in nature, or cultivating qualities such as truthfulness or compassion. If you're a busy mother, your meditation time might be the two minutes before everybody wakes up, and your "time in nature" might consist of being present with the trees while you watch your children at the playground. At a different stage of life you might have thirty minutes or more each day to devote to your spiritual path.

Where are you right now in your path? Is it working for you?

Levels of Soul Purpose

SIMPLY TO BE

The first level of soul purpose is simply to be. Soul wishes to experience itself in the physical reality and still be simply soul. In our striving world, this must be emphasized again and again. At a core level nothing needs to be done. Behind the feeling of karma is perfect existence.

SELF KARMA AND KARMA WITH OTHERS

The second level of soul purpose relates to karmic energies we created while incarnated in prior lives. Even though we are perfect on a soul level, once we incarnate into the physical realm, we get ourselves into various challenging situations because we have forgotten who we are. Lifetime after lifetime our karma accumulates. The Buddhist would say this is like a shadow in front of the sun. It can be seen as the black and dense energy of unresolved experience embedded energetically in our chakras and aura.

Karma can be defined as action and reaction. I think of it as the sum total of all unresolved emotional or energetic experience brought into our current incarnation. Unresolved experiences are held in the aura as energy and are taken from one life to another, dematerializing in death and materializing into the next incarnation. It is a perfect system that allows us to repeat, heal or change as we choose. There is generally too much karmic energy to be cleared in one life, despite a lament I hear from time to time—a wish this would be one's last life. However, if we had to clear all of our karma in one life it would be way too challenging. So, only a part of it is ripening in each incarnation.

Our karma may be defined as "self-karma," meaning it's quite personal. It is our own pattern and not related to someone else. We may work it out with another, but at a deep level, we are aware this is our personal repetitive pattern we wish to master.

If the karma is related to others, there may be specific souls with whom we wish to work things out. We will have soul agreements to be in relationship for this purpose. These relationships often feel quite fated and we feel thrilled to meet one of these soul friends. This can be confusing when the relationship "doesn't turn out" when we felt such a deep soul connection and bond from the moment our eyes, known as "the windows to the soul," connected with each other.

Karma may be considered "good" or "bad" by the mind, which tries to categorize everything, but there is no need for karma judgment. It is just energy that is stuck in a groove and needs to be resolved in some way and released. Karma can also be well-deserved gifts. But many times karma is simply repetitive. We do the same things repetitively, needing to learn to change the pattern and break free.

You might have a karma from an action against another. You stole a loaf of bread. Now you receive that action back (your bicycle is stolen, your credit card is hacked) so that you understand your actions more clearly. You feel the feeling you caused to another. Simple action/reaction.

I imagine that most of you reading this can't imagine killing another human. You might not kill insects. Perhaps you've decided it's immoral to eat animals or use animal products. How did you come to this consciousness? You have experienced both (or many) sides of complex moral issues. You have learned to respect life, yet life is complex. What if you see a black widow spider and your baby daughter is on the floor? What if you live in a remote area where animal protein is the only available sustenance? There are endless karmic gray areas we wrestle with.

Deeper karmic issues involve loss of life or free will. Over many lives we learn to harness the intensity of our anger and rage to avoid true harm to others. We learn this through creating harm and being harmed, or by atoning and helping many people, like a surgeon who travels to disadvantaged countries every year to help impoverished children. Or you may have helped many individuals in the past and now they are eager to offer generosities when they meet you. This is all the nature of learning through karmic experience.

When we are in a challenging situation, we often do not know the phase of the karma we find ourselves in. Is this the beginning of a relationship with someone and we are creating something new? Is this an old karmic pattern? The truth is, it is unlikely that new karma is being created at this point in your lives. You have most likely done this dance with the beloved over and over again. When I say "beloved" I don't mean the people you think you love. If someone is showing up strongly in your life, even as an "enemy," on a soul level there is deep connection. Everyone you meet is a teacher, and a beloved. (Ouch, I know that's hard to imagine with some of the "beloved enemies" with whom you are struggling).

Who started it? Who owes who? You may never know, although this is where the exploration of past lives through meditation and regression can help.

No matter who started the karmic story, you can get in touch with your spiritual inner wisdom and make a choice that is filled with integrity, compassion and kindness. It's never a karmic mistake to operate from solid spiritual principles. This includes having compassion for ourselves, so we do not have to suffer or be martyred by our karma.

As we work through various life situations with integrity, responsibility and awareness, allowing ourselves to feel the feelings, we begin to heal the karmic story. With integration and re-lease of emotions such as fear, shame, guilt, grief and pain, the karma will be released and a greater connection to joy, bliss, ac-ceptance and surrender will be realized.

Mission in the World

The third type of soul purpose might be a mission in the world. This can present as a highly visible calling or one that you ex-press in a way that looks like a more "quiet life"—it doesn't mat-ter. This is our service to others. Perhaps your soul purpose is more professional and seems monetary or non-spiritual. Some souls are here to learn about money and power. Not everyone is here to be famous or to live a life driven by spiritual pursuit. You might need to open your mind and accept where your heart is drawn to understand your worldly soul purpose.

No matter what level of mission or karmic pattern you're working with, the first step, and perhaps most important to all spiritual endeavors, is meditation. Meditation of some type is a foundational activity to develop the Spiritual Pillar of your life.

REFLECTION #9

1. Journal Reflection:
Consider your capacity simply to "be"—imagining you don't need to accomplish anything.

Then contemplate your life from the perspective of self-karma lessons, karma with others in relationships, and a sense of calling in the world.

Breathe into the various thoughts and feelings and ask "what is asked of me now?"

2. Journal Reflection: Contemplate and journal about your spiritual path throughout your whole life, including how it is now. Where have you felt connected to Spirit? (Nature, church, in meditation, with children . . . etc.)

In your spiritual path (church, meditation, nature, service, etc.), do you have the tendency toward discipline? If so, do you find yourself overcommitting and then drifting away from the rigidity? Or do you stick with it no matter what, perhaps feeling burdened or resentful? Or do you feel balanced and comfortable with your practice?

Or, is your tendency to do what you want when you want, a more eclectic path that may not have a focus?

Either way: What do you like about your current spiritual path? What would you like to add, release, change?

3. Journal Reflection: When you think about your spiritual path in connection to the Mission Statement you've written and the analysis of the Karmic Story and the Twelve areas of life, how would a deeper connection to your spiritual nature, Spirit guides or High Self, help you now?

CHAPTER TEN

Spiritual/Meditation

"We tend to think of meditation in only one
way. But life itself is a meditation."
—Raul Julia

Many people have told me they *"tried"* meditation and it didn't *"work"* for them. It was too hard. They couldn't stay focused. They couldn't concentrate. Their bodies hurt.

Yes exactly.

This is how it is.

It isn't easy to meditate in the beginning. Probably it isn't easy to meditate in the middle or in the end, either. Most people find meditation challenging, especially in fast-paced and frenzied Western cultures. It's as if we need "pre-meditation" time: to learn to breathe deeply, to be in touch with the current moment, to slow thoughts down. After learning to relax a little, we can set our sights on meditating for very short periods of time.

Meditation requires patience. It's called a meditation "practice" because it is never accomplished.

You don't have to meditate in an uncomfortable seated yoga posture or struggle to meditate for long periods at the beginning; you can ease into your practice. With sustained practice you might find yourself looking forward to your meditation. Of course, maybe not. Even seasoned meditators will go through periods of resistance.

Meditation calms and balances the body, and clears the mind to facilitate intuitive opening. Meditation also creates quiet space to allow for an opening to Spirit. With time it becomes a significant part of a spiritual path.

The simplicity of focused breathing allows you to drop in, to be present to the moment. This feels easier or harder depending on the day, just like the ups and downs of life. With time, the ritual of repetition becomes familiar. When you sit on your cushion or your favorite meditation chair you can feel a collective (body/mind/spirit) sigh of relief. You will discover that each time you sit the experience is unique, like a snowflake.

Often we begin with an intention to accomplish something through meditation, like better intuition or a quieter mind, or lower blood pressure. With time we appreciate the journey. We accept the challenge of sitting and relish the moments of calm centering.

If you know nature is your doorway to spirituality, you can combine time outside with meditation for your unique practice.

Here are some suggestions for a pre-meditation warm up. Every day take a few deep breaths. Learn to expand and relax the belly with each inhale. Most of us have a tendency to hold our bellies pulled in, hoping we look oh-so thin. This causes us to breathe shallow upper chest breaths. Practice yoga or simple stretches to open up the hips, thighs and low back. Look for opportunities to focus mindfully on one task at a time.

When you are ready, you can try a simple classic meditation. Place your body in a position with the spine straight. Traditionally, this is seated cross-legged or in a lotus position for those with more open yoga hips. Cultures with a long history of meditation are often those who sit cross-legged or squat in daily life. Most Westerners sit in chairs for long periods and have tight hips and hamstrings.

Thus, *"find a comfortable position"* means that the position should be comfortable for your body as it is in this moment. Initially you might sit in a chair with your feet flat on the floor (if you need to be more grounded) or with your feet crossed (this will feel less grounded but perhaps more attuned to higher energies. Experiment).

You can also lie down. This is not traditional, but if this is very comfortable for you and you have difficulty sitting, *"find a comfortable position"* may mean you lie down. This will be a good starting point.

Hand positions can vary. You can place your hands in any one of these positions:

1. Rest hands gently on thighs, palms up (to awakening) or down (for grounding).

2. Rest backs of hands on your legs with the thumb and pointer finger gently touching.

3. Rest hands gently in your lap, nondominant hand cradling under your dominant hand, palms up.

Then you breathe. Of course you are already breathing, but there is a difference between the unconscious natural breathing we do 24/7 and a conscious, deep, slow breath. As you focus your attention on your breath, allow the breath to settle into a gentle, slow rhythm that feels natural to you. Breathe in and out through the nose or in through the nose and out through the mouth. The tongue rests softly at the top of the palate, just behind the teeth. Soften and expand the belly with each inhale. When you exhale there is a natural contraction inward of the belly.

Whenever you notice you have started to drift off or think about anything, gently bring yourself back to your breath, noticing the inhale and exhale. Do not fight the thinking process, simply pay less and less attention to it, allowing the breath to be the focal point of attention. You can also use the flame of a candle, a mantra (repeated word/s), sacred art object, or a flower as a focal point of attention. You will still stay connected to the breath rhythm even with this visual point of attention.

Begin with five minutes. Set a timer so you don't have to open your eyes to look at the clock. Add extra minutes as you feel more comfortable. Ten to twenty minutes a day is a good initial goal. If you have time and inclination for thirty to sixty minutes of daily meditation, this devotion to practice can be life-altering.

Listen to your intuition. Find a practice of meditation that works with your life, as it is, now. Start where you are.

Troubleshooting

1. YOU FALL ASLEEP WHEN YOU MEDITATE.

Falling asleep is understandable when you first begin to meditate. Most people work too hard, move too fast or drink too much caffeine. When you sit and breathe this may be the first time your body has relaxed in years. Be easy on yourself. Know that falling asleep allows you to continue relaxing into the sleep state, and don't use this as a reason to give up. The Dalai Lama gives you permission: *"Sleep is the best meditation."*

If you attempt to meditate in the morning when you're still tired, or in the evening before bed, of course you're more likely to fall asleep. Try meditating in the middle of the day when you feel more awake. If you don't feel rested and awake at any time of the day, you can surrender to the idea of meditation napping. As your spiritual practice leads you to physical mindfulness and deeper levels of healing, you might catch up on sleep and be able to meditate more easily without sleeping.

2. YOU ARE VERY FIDGETY AND UNABLE TO STOP THINKING.

Are you a person who tends to fidget, loves to clean the house, mow the lawn, work out, and generally can't sit for very long without jumping up to do the next activity? If so, you might be "moving centered." Moving-centered people need regular physical activity more than most. The most basic moving meditation is walking meditation. You can do this outside on your favorite simple walking trail or on a treadmill. I say *simple* walking trail because dodging rocks, dogs and steep cliffs doesn't easily support the focused, steady breath.

Breathe steadily in alignment with each step. Breathe in with a step and breathe out with a step. Perhaps with a deep slow breath you can walk two or three steps per breath. It's a bit like swimming where you choose how many strokes your arms make between each breath. Simply pace your strides to the breath. You can also jog, run or ride a bike in alignment with rhythmic breath.

Try not to go on a rampage of uncontrolled thinking. This is not the time to ponder problems in detail. Gently ignore thoughts, imagining them floating away on the breeze. You might also enjoy yoga and Tai Chi—two well-developed forms of moving meditation that will be discussed more in the section on the physical.

3. THOUGHTS JUST WON'T LET GO.

The grocery list, friends and random task ideas will keep interrupting you at the beginning. Again, this is normal. Bring your attention back to the breath and allow the thoughts to release gently. Do not engage with thoughts; do not actively push them away.

If this doesn't work for you and the thoughts are continually distracting, you can keep a pad of paper and a pen next to you to write the persistent thoughts down. Then go right back to the breath. After a while you'll learn to think less and to be less driven to take thought seriously.

Thoughts are the ego's way of trying to prevent you from this new activity that will connect you to Spirit and minimize the ego/mind hold on your life and self-concept. It is often a small (or gigantic) battle in the beginning.

4. THE THOUGHTS STILL WON'T LET GO!

Guided meditations and visualizations can give your mind something to do and are healing in a different way than quiet, seated meditation. Guided meditations to cleanse and align the chakras can also help purify and balance your energy system, which leads to an easier time in basic breath meditations.

Ultimate Meditation

Once you have mastered the ability to breathe and the mind has begun to calm down, you may find you are able to hold a meditative deep awareness of all energy and form, inside and out, with eyes open. This is discussed by the Tantric scholar Christopher "Hareesh" Wallis (author of *Tantra Illuminated*).

I found that after many years of meditation I experienced long periods of time without much thought of any kind. I could sit and perceive and breathe without mental distraction. I didn't know this was the goal, and I don't really know when it started. The process unfolded gradually over five or ten years. At first my mind moved from persistent thinking with moments of calm through meditation, to lengthier periods of calm and "no-thought" awareness punctuated by surprising intervals of mental activity. Of course, if you're in a meditation and you notice you're not thinking, then suddenly you actually are thinking about not thinking. Then a thinking loop begins and the moment is lost.

Hareesh says that the original meaning of the word "meditation" was this state of awareness and perception without thinking or judging. Everything we normally think of as meditation, such as the classic meditation instruction discussed above, might more accurately be considered pre-meditation—a process of learning how to breathe and still the mind. It takes time to be able to practice this true or ultimate meditation that might be described as complete awareness.

It's complex and so very simple. Start where you are with breath and a comfortable position. Your practice will evolve. Practice to infinity.

Cultivation of "Spiritual" Qualities

Do you remember the first time you understood the concept of spirituality, separate from religion? It is certainly possible to be nurtured and supported by the structure of religion, finding spirituality that is meaningful to you within it. Spirituality might be more personal and unique to your own experience. Your church might take many forms. You might find Spirit on the floor of a yoga studio, by the ocean, hiking through a forest, or through the vibrant light of the sun.

I still remember when I first heard reincarnation discussed. I was sixteen years old. An older friend mentioned reincarnation and my ears perked up. The word was interesting. She said that we get reborn again and again into different bodies and different lives. And I thought, *"Oh yeah, that's right!"* It felt like a relief to hear truth that wasn't much part of the culture at the time. Spiritual concepts can meet with our resistance, curiosity or questioning, or there can be an initial moment of resonance—a sense that what you are hearing is true, and maybe even strangely familiar.

Absolute belief isn't necessary. A spiritual path emerges as you live it, observing what is true for you. Your path is unique. Many spiritual teachers from various disciplines will suggest you pick one path—one lineage or one teacher—and stick to it for maximum benefit. Although that seems like a clear and direct path, many of us do try a few spiritual roads or attempt to integrate two or more belief systems. *Jewish Buddhists? Christian Yogis?*

All paths come together in agreement about a list of spiritual qualities to ponder andcultivate and/or a list of things not to do. The Ten Commandments of Christianity, The Torah of Judaism, The Yamas and the Niyamas of Yoga Philosophy, the Quran of Islam . . . Belief systems throughout centuries have listed spiritual goals for those who wish to follow the system.

These beliefs converge and differ. There's a general consensus about love, compassion, forgiveness, honesty, generosity—qualities we easily recognize as "spiritual." We usually wish to have more of these—from our own actions and from those around us—and feel good inside when we live them authentically.

What is harder to understand are the non-dual spiritual traditions that suggest everything, absolutely everything, is part of Spirit embodied. Therefore even the most unpleasant qualities of anger, hatred, rage, jealousy and attachment are part of a spiritual experience in the physical realm and cannot be disowned or repressed without consequences.

Even more exotic to experience is the deep, quiet place behind and within both "positive" spiritual traits and "negative" spiritual traits where there is stillness, no thought, and no feeling.

A spiritual path allows us to explore and experience the amazing levels of possibility of life, including feelings and no feelings.

Some spiritual traditions discourage seekers from developing their intuitive abilities because the ego can get fixated on this way of receiving information. Intuitive input can become a mind trip if we focus on controlling or preparing for all of life's events, and avoid the deeper levels of true spiritual awareness. Some religions caution against psychic awareness because of a historical belief that the information is from dark sources or even the "devil."

I honor these concerns, yet respectfully disagree. Intuition is a natural and powerful inner guidance tool available to all, as much a part of us humans as talking or breathing. It is a gift that can help us navigate life. We use it all of the time whether we know it or not. I suggest that we learn to do it well rather than pretend we're not using it, scrambling to figure things out with mental process—which is definitely not a spiritual tool, but rather in service to the ego/mind.

Intuition is spiritual in nature because it acts as a bridge between the physical and the unseen world of Spirit and energy. Through intuition we can listen more clearly to our hearts. We can receive clear inner guidance and feel a deeper sense of meaning in life. It is an amazing tool. Intuition is not, however, a spiritual path. We are not being spiritual, or necessarily evolving, when we are psychic. It is simply one part of living a spiritually-infused life.

REFLECTION #10

1. Meditation: Consider a realistic schedule and length of time for meditation. Commit to your meditation practice and perhaps journal about your experiences. Cultivate meditation as a habit, like brushing your teeth. Five minutes is better than striving to do an hour but never getting to it.

CHAPTER ELEVEN

Intuition

*"There is no logical way to the discovery of these elemental laws.
There is only the way of intuition, which is helped by a
feeling for the order lying behind the appearance."*
—Albert Einstein

The phone rings. You already know who is calling. It's like a
flash in your mind. You're not quite sure, but as soon as you
pick up the phone and hear the voice of your best friend, you
know you *did know* just seconds before the phone rang. And then
you remember you dreamed about her last night. It was like you
were two heads face-to-face. The bottom of your bodies seemed
filmy—maybe not even there. The memory of the dream is very
light and ethereal. You might not have even remembered it if she
hadn't just called. But she was in the dream, sitting across from
you, telling you she was going to move to another state. Was it
Rhode Island?

Now she's actually on the phone, telling you she's moving to
a new job in Boston, and not sure where she'll live, maybe Rhode

Island. It's weird. You talk about it. Have a laugh. And then you go back to not being sure how intuitive you are, perhaps imagining other people have special powers. You might not understand how you get intuitive information, or you might not trust it, but it is there for you sometimes.

As our culture shifts toward openness and connectivity, there is greater acceptance and awareness of our natural intuitive abilities. We may use the word "psychic," which implies specific information and vision, or "intuitive"—a word that seems less elite and implies inner knowing, feelings or a natural sense of what's true for us. Either way, the ability to access, deepen and clarify intuition is becoming a necessary skill in life.

Everyone has the capacity to be intuitive or psychic, to receive information from Spirit guides and to know or sense truth that is in alignment with Self. It is also possible to know what happens before it occurs, although as we deepen in our understanding of life, we often find ourselves less interested in knowing the future and more interested in using these gifts simply as a compass—to know when we are aligned with our path.

As you learn more about your natural abilities, they can be incredibly useful for everyday life. In this section you will learn more about the different types of intuitive skills. You don't have to have special talent to do this; you're using intuition all the time without realizing it. Intuition is a typical part of the decision-making process. You might "feel" one way about something even though you think something different. You might "see" a direction for yourself even though you feel rather blocked about how to get there.

All day long we are bombarded by messages received on the subtle levels. To go through life without learning how to clarify these messages and trust this amazing source of guidance is to walk through the streets blindfolded.

Are you psychic?

The word psychic sometimes calls up a picture of a gypsy sitting at the side of the road, doing something magical and slightly suspicious, or a slightly unusual person helping the police find a missing person. Yet there isn't a strong difference between being psychic and intuitive. It's probably a matter of degree and your comfort with the words. "Psychic" tends to imply specific details and awareness, amazing predictions or knowledge. So although we might use the words psychic and intuitive interchangeably, "intuitive" feels like a safer label. Most of us can agree that we are intuitive at least some of the time. And the shift to the acceptance of intuition is particularly stunning in the corporate world.

> *". . . And most important, have the courage*
> *to follow your heart and intuition."*
> — Steve Jobs

Since around the year 2000, when our world shifted into a higher vibration, business gurus have been talking and writing more frequently about intuition and "emotional intelligence" as core skills for success. This was not the case decades ago when emphasis was on analysis and cold, hard facts. Books like Gary Klein's *The Power of Intuition: How to Use your Gut Feelings to Make Decisions at Work* and William Dugan's *Strategic Intuition* are published with increasing frequency and credibility.

Beyond basic strategies for intuitive development, a basic understanding of the chakra system and the various ways we receive information can help you understand how you are receiving subtle information already—what your core skills naturally are—and how to develop and clarify them further. Chakras are swirling vortexes of energy within the human energy field that are part of an elegant communication system.

There are five major building blocks to cultivating intuitive wisdom:

MEDITATION

Meditation is essential to clear the mind for intuitive development. Not only does meditation help you build spiritual awareness, it is probably *the most important step* to attain clarity. Our ego-driven thoughts and fears can create a mental clutter that confuses us. We are unable to hear the voices of our guides or trust our insights.

You can use any meditation style designed to create a clear and unattached mind. This includes Tai Chi, yoga or meditative walking. Guided visualization styles of meditation to visually and energetically clear the aura and chakras (as we will do in the reflection section) are also beneficial.

SPIRIT CONNECTION

We all have Spirit guides—usually at least three or more. They give us information that we initially perceive as our own thoughts. With meditation and practice, a more specific connection with Spirit guides or Higher Self can be developed to receive accurate and clear information. It may be helpful to have guidance and support from a spiritual teacher or take a training to learn to connect with high-level Spirits safely and clearly. Begin by connecting to one guide who proves itself to be of the Light— both clear and accurate—before being introduced by that guide to others. Connecting to any voice that cares to speak to you is a dangerous practice. As they say, "just because they're dead, they're not necessarily smart." Or nice, I would add. There are many different kinds and levels of guides. It's important to seek high-level and spiritually grounded sources of information.

EMOTIONAL CLARITY

In order to be intuitively clear, it is helpful to observe, understand and maintain your cleanest emotional state possible. It is challenging to receive clear information when you are stressed or feeling strong emotions like anger or grief. Your empathic/feeling receptors might be clogged with your own feelings or the feelings of others.

PHYSICAL CLARITY

You will be clearer when your body is strong and healthy. Poor health creates a fogginess that spreads into your personal psychic realm. Each person has a unique constitution, so there is no one recipe for health. Observe and modify your personal physical needs such as diet, exercise regimen, supplements, alcohol and other substances (including sugar and caffeine), as well as sleep. We know these factors affect health, and they also affect our ability to be a clear channel for information and healing energies.

PRACTICE, PRACTICE, PRACTICE

You can use opportunities in daily life to ask questions of Spirit guides. You can also make a habit of checking in with your kinesthetic intuition or "gut feeling" as often as you can. "How do I actually feel emotionally now?" "How is my body feeling now?" "What do I most truly need right now?"

You can also ask simple, mundane questions of your guides for practice. Spirit guides are much like loving friends who are willing to help us with simple problems so we can ultimately focus on deeper and more complex choices. Once we learn to trust the answers to simple daily questions, when we have a real crisis or emergency for which trusted guidance is essential, we will have a sense of what an accurate exchange feels like and be able to trust the answer.

Practice questions might be *"Will my friend actually follow through on lunch plans this week?"* Or *"What lesson should I be aware of today?"* Ideally if you meditate in the morning when you are mentally and psychically most clear each day, you can immediately write a few things down in your journal, noting your perceived sense of connection or clarity.

Through this daily self-practice, you get to know the difference between when you are accurate and clear and when your thoughts and emotions affect accuracy. This will refine your skill.

By developing intuition, over time you purify the mind to embody a greater sense of clarity, peace and inner harmony. It's not a spiritual path, but the same practices and skills develop both intuition and spiritual nature. These practices help us to live in rapidly changing times with a deeper sense of trust in our path.

Do You Have Muscles? You Also Have Chakras

I like to compare psychic skills to athletic skills. Everyone has muscles, yet some people are not drawn to physical activity at all, barely using their muscles except to do what is necessary to move around. Others will enjoy a little activity, and with practice and exercise might develop a good tennis game or enjoy a brisk run, a walk on the treadmill or a Zumba class. Yet there are those who are born with athletic gifts. They have the drive to be physical and competitive, and they seem coordinated or balanced even as young children. With dedication, practice and coaching, these more gifted children might develop into professional athletes.

And so it is with psychic abilities. All humans have the same chakra system that transmits and receives energetic information. Chakras are swirling vortexes of energy that begin along the spinal column and swirl in every larger circles through the body surface and out into the aura, the electromagnetic energy field around and through each of us. Chakras are important receptors and transmitters of subtle information. They facilitate our subconscious awareness of safety, intuition, feelings and telepathic conversations. They can be naturally open and strong, or closed, blocked or repressed. With learning and practice, we can develop a greater degree of awareness of how the chakras work. This clarity leads to natural awareness in day-to-day life and enhanced intuitive abilities.

Victoria was a classic intuitive person, who came to me not at all sure about "how all of this works."

"I get premonitions or dreams about things sometimes, but when I need the information I don't know how to get it. I also don't usually know where it's coming from and I don't know whether I should trust it," she said. "I keep thinking I'm just making this stuff up in my head, but then often it turns out to be true. Sometimes I get very accurate and clear information but then sometimes I'm completely off. I don't know how to get consistently accurate information, and bottom line, I want to be able to trust what I get . . ."

As you learn to open and clarify your intuition, it is helpful to have opportunities to practice with people you don't know, or don't know well. It is the most difficult to get information for yourself, especially when you are emotionally upset about something. It is a little easier to get information for a friend. And it is usually much easier to get information for a complete stranger than a friend. The more ideas and opinions you have in your mind, the harder it is to be a clear channel of information.

THIS IS A NATURAL ABILITY . . .

Everyone is psychic, and if we had been encouraged as children to trust our feelings and visions and to know that our imaginary friends were our Spirit guides, it wouldn't be so challenging to open back up again. The study of intuition is like going back to elementary school to remind us of what we already know and or what skills we have developed in prior lives. Once we have remembered how to use our natural intuitive gifts we'll find that life flows more easily—as it is meant to.

Four Psychic Pathways

Now we'll explore the four different psychic pathways. In the reflection section there will be a brief exercise for you to determine which of the four pathways feels most comfortable to you, although all can be developed. I'll help you discover whether you are a visual "seer," auditory "telepath," a feeling empath or a direct channel—or a combination of two or more of these.

1. Clairsentience & Empathy

Clairsentience is the ability to feel energy clearly and to receive knowledge about another person or the environment through your emotional and body-level perceptions. You are using general clairsentient skill when you pick up feelings just being around people—anger, fear, depression, etc.. If you sense even more detail in this way perhaps your aptitude is stronger.

Clairsentience can be activated through psychometry, the process of holding an object belonging to another person. This skill is demonstrated by psychics who help the police find missing people. The psychic holds a piece of jewelry or an article of clothing frequently worn by the missing person. The vibration of the item acts as a conduit to the vibration of the person; pictures, words and feelings are sensed by the psychic.

Clairsentience is occurring spontaneously if you:

- *Feel tired or confused in large groups of people*

- *Find your mood changes when you are standing near total strangers*

- *Have your friends tell you that they always feel much better after talking to you, but you feel tired and drained*

- *Are easily affected by feelings and activities in films. (They cry, you cry. They eat a sandwich, you suddenly want a sandwich.)*

The second chakra in the lower abdomen is the primary clairsentient receptor, but people with strong clairsentience often have a weak and ragged aura, especially on the left side. While psychic opening usually involves opening chakras, you will need to close your second chakra to some degree, especially when in groups of people. You will need to fortify and rebuild the left side of the aura to hold and maintain energy and boundaries.

How do you rebuild a side of an aura? Through meditation (just can't get away from it). Visualization combined with the power of your intention can change the state of your aura and chakras.

Empathy is the ability to understand and be sensitive to another person's thoughts and feelings. It is not the same as sympathy, which is a less useful emotion of feeling sorry for another's experience or sad for their feelings. Empathy is the gift of knowing another person without them explicitly communicating to you. Likewise, the recipient of empathy will feel understood and "seen" without that being expressed. If you are an empathic person you probably seem like a good listener. That's because you're listening with your emotional antennae as well as your ears. As you listen empathically, you reflect back to the person both what they're saying and what you're perceiving about the real underlying emotions: "I know you're feeling furious about this situation but I *can feel* that you're also scared about what's going to happen."

Many of us do this naturally in daily conversations, empathizing and understanding truth through our clairsentient skills. As you accept that you do this, if you slow down the process and listen even more closely to the emotional intuitive clues you receive from others, you refine this skill. You are less likely to be shocked by other people's actions and behaviors. You can learn to communicate about what is truly going on and not act as if the surface words are true. Empathy and clairsentience allow you to be real in your relationships.

When your empathy and clairsentience are fully developed, you can know detailed, accurate information about another person. It is less likely you will use this as a psychic skill to know about your own life, although empathy for yourself is part of a healing path.

Jessica was a sensitive and friendly girl, an immediate friend to everyone she met, rescuing spiders and moths, bringing home stray dogs. As she approached puberty, she began to put on some extra weight, typical of preteens. At first her mom wasn't worried at all, believing it was a natural phase. However, as the weight continued to climb, alarming her pediatrician, Jessica also began to dread going to school. "*I feel everything, Mom!*" she said. "*Yesterday I was sitting in history class and my leg started hurting really bad. Angie was sitting next to me and then she told me she had fallen off her bike and hurt her leg—the same leg that was hurting me.*"

Is this you? Or maybe a young person you know?

Soon Jessica didn't want to go to school at all. No amount of cajoling, rewards or restrictions could motivate her to sit in a room of teenagers who were filled with various emotional and physical ailments.

All of our psychic sensitivities increase around puberty, adding to the challenge of this time of transition. Extra weight can be one way the body tries to add psychic protection to make up for penetrable psychic boundaries, a hallmark of clairsentient people.

2. Clairaudience: Clear Hearing

Clairaudience or "clear hearing" is the intuitive listening skill. It is the whisper of a voice in your head that you might mistake for a thought. Sometimes the hearing isn't so clear; clairaudience can include a symphony of thoughts from others heard streaming through your brain. This intuitive talent allows you to hear the various voices of Spirit guides.

To clarify your clairaudient skill, you need to calm your mind so your thinking isn't out of control, random and repetitive. With time you will recognize the subtle differences between your thoughts and psychic conversations.

Psychic communication is normal for everyone, whether you believe in it or not. It is not necessary to believe in bone marrow because you've never seen it, but it's inside of you and is a part of your body. Your capacity for hearing and sending energetic communications is part of your energy body. It is happening throughout the day, and the night. The back-and-forth of this subtle thought communication can also be called telepathy. We talk telepathically with people we know, and also with animals and spirits. The fifth chakra (throat) is the receptor for clairaudience.

When you first listen for messages using this high-frequency hearing sense, you will have a unique experience of what the "voice" sounds like. Often you'll hear Spirit communication as if it is a conversation in your own brain. You might realize quite unexpectedly a conversation has been chattering away in your mind for a few seconds while you weren't paying much attention. It's as if you're suddenly listening in.

Margaret's husband died of a heart attack. Stunned, she contacted me because she was desperate to know he was okay, and to have communication with him. She told me she thought she was having trouble letting go of him, because she would realize she was talking to him in her mind. She would find herself asking him questions about what to do about finances, the gardener, or other daily choices she felt overwhelmed about. She would hear his answer in her thoughts and then notice this mental conversation. Margaret tried to shake off these conversations as craziness. But this was the Spirit communication she hoped to have. She just didn't realize it.

Validation might occur when you notice your guides speak with a different vocabulary or use a different cadence or rhythm in their speech. People imagine they're making things up, but often guides will give you messages that you would never even think of. Over time you will notice the difference between the messages your mind thinks of as random thoughts and the messages you receive from Spirit.

One way to know you're thinking and not receiving intuitive messages is because you are actually thinking . . . a lot. If you are thinking about a problem—ruminating, anxious, stressed or frightened—you are most likely caught in an endless thought loop. It is rare you could possibly hear messages from Spirit when your brain is caught in monkey mind. Even if Spirits are trying to talk to you, they can't get a word in edgewise.

Often a Spirit message arrives with a "thud." One moment you're spacing out or walking down the street (or spacing out while walking down the street), and then suddenly you hear a voice in your mind that is clear and strong. It might be about a completely different subject than what you were last thinking about, or it could be a random new idea regarding a current topic of thought.

As I approached a complex writing project I was wondering if I should move onto a houseboat to focus on writing, or if I should stay where I was to avoid the disruption of a move, or possibly move elsewhere (definitely a mental thought process). Suddenly a voice in my mind said, "This needs to be complete by April." The voice felt sure and true, and the feeling resonated in my belly. I had the feeling I could choose where I lived during this time period, and the thought process about place instantly stopped.

The next step was for me to decide how I could most easily complete the work by April, and also to consider or ask Spirit to define April of what year. I've learned that the hard way. Best not to jump to conclusions about general answers. Technically April could refer to April in any year at all.

Here's another story about how the voice of Spirit guided Ginger:

Ginger is an amazing animal lover with a heart of pure love. Anyone would want to come back in another life as one of her well-cared-for cats. Her natural intuition is very strong, often leading her to take unusual routes or leave home at times that don't make sense in her normal schedule. As she follows this profound inner guidance, quite often she will find a bird or an animal in distress that she takes immediately to the emergency vet or wild animal rescue. Over time, she has learned to trust these inner impulses, although she still has a fairly strong inner critic voice that tells her she's crazy. As so often we do.

This time the intuition came as she went to feed the stray cats that live in the center of town, a daily task.

She said, "I went to the opposite lot than where I park normally, which required walking further to the feeding place. It seemed odd to me as I did it. I noticed one car in the lot, and after feeding the cats, I noticed an old lady sitting in the car on the opposite side of the lot. A voice said "go over." "I did," she said. I asked her if she was okay, because the medical offices were closed. She started crying. She had been stuck since noon. Her car died after her doctor appointment, and the doors automatically lock to the medical buildings for security. She had hip surgery and couldn't walk far to get help anyway. So to help, I called her daughter who then came to get her."

The voice that said "go over" was a voice inside of her head, not much different than a thought, except that it had a stronger, directive tone, a voice she has learned to recognize as a Spirit guide, a voice to be listened to.

When you begin to hear your guides you may find they give a lot of information all at once. You may also experience the exact opposite: you get one word or a short phrase. When too much information comes at once it's like a cascading waterfall and can be hard to remember. Have a quick way to write down or record what you receive. In the old days I'd say keep a notebook handy. Now you'll likely have a smart phone with a note-taking app and a recording app. You can speak or write everything you're hearing. When the clairaudient information arrives slowly or is just a few words or phrases, it is easy to feel discouraged. You might feel you're not doing it right. It's helpful to remember that in the beginning, that's either all the Spirits can communicate at a time or it is all you are able receive.

It's amazing that a disembodied Spirit can communicate anything to us at all. They are invisible, energetic beings formulating language via energetic impulse transmissions. We might assume it's no big deal for them to be able to transmit messages, but the reality is some Spirits are more skilled than others. Some improve their communication clarity over time as we also learn to develop our inner listening skills.

Clairaudience is generally an internal brain voice but it can also be ferociously loud and strong—as if you are hearing it through your ears as a normal voice. You might assume a person has spoken when you heard their thoughts as a voice. Occasionally in a very dangerous situation your guides will "yell" to get your attention.

Kathy's son had died when he was thirty years old, a loss nearly impossible for any mother to recover from. She would come to see me once in a while to check on him and was soothed to receive Spirit messages from him and about him, but always wished to have more of a sense of his presence personally. One summer she went on a whitewater rafting trip that changed everything for her.

"We hit some particularly turbulent water and I was tossed out of the raft. Everything happened so fast, but right away I heard Danny's voice yell 'Mom!' As the force of the river swept me along, banging into rocks and branches, I could feel him with me. I was trying to grab onto something, but he told me to fold my hands across the center of my chest, which I did," she said.

"I would catch some air and be on top and then be pulled under again. Finally I was totally exhausted, dragged under water again, and I told him I just couldn't do it anymore. He encouraged me to hang on and told me very clearly that I could keep going, that I was going to come up and I'd be okay."

She continued, "When the Search and Rescue team found me I was five miles down the river from where I'd fallen out. Frankly, they were looking for a dead body. They were shocked to find me alive, and with my hands still firmly clasped over my chest. They wondered how I knew how to get in that position, which is apparently the way to survive in a river like that so that your arms don't get caught on a rock or under a log. That's how most people die in these rivers. My son saved me, and I knew absolutely for sure after that that he really was okay and that he was still with me."

Although Kathy was in a dangerous situation requiring the Spirit of her son to yell powerfully to get her attention, most of the time the psychic information received through clairaudience comes more subtly. With practice you'll be able to discern the difference between real voices and your thoughts.

Meditation is always the answer.

Meditation clears the mind so you will receive information clearly and accurately. If your mind is cluttered, the information will still be there, waiting for you, but you may not "read" the messages. It's as if your inbox is full, stacked with papers, messy and disorganized. There are times when the ability to have a clear mind and hear the messages in the moment can be crucial. Regular mental housekeeping prepares you for the unexpected.

For me, one critical event occurred on a vacation trip in Panama. My husband at the time and I had taken a canoe trip up a river to spend time with an indigenous tribe. It was a sweltering hot day, and they suggested we could swim in the river. As a couple of friends sat chatting on the sand near the edge of the river, we waded out into the apparently calm and shallow water. I noticed as I tried swimming that when I swam against the current I couldn't make any forward progress. The strength of the current was deceiving. It was like one of those endless home lap pools—I kept swimming upstream but not getting anywhere.

Meanwhile my adventurous husband had crossed the river and was standing chest deep near the other shore, preparing to walk downstream toward birds he had discovered. Suddenly, a voice in my head said, "Go and get him to come back, he's going to get into trouble over there." My attention was directed to an area down the river on the same side I was standing on. It was as if a spotlight was focused on this area. It lit up visually to me.

Despite this very clear and direct message, I didn't feel comfortable telling him what to do. Knowing him to be an independent spirit, I argued with this voice in my head. "No, I don't want to be that controlling." I wondered briefly if he was at risk of a heart attack and if that was the possible trouble. "Get him to come back," the voice repeated. "Go and help him!"

"Why don't you come back over to this sandy side?" I called to him tentatively. The inner Spirit push to be by his side was insistent. Reluctantly I started across to meet him and we then crossed back, the increasingly strong current pulling us downstream. As we neared the riverbank, he disappeared suddenly under the water, caught in the center of a churning water vortex. One more step and I would be in it too. I now realized we were in the area I had seen lit up. The current had pushed us down river even as we thought we were crossing directly. I now caught sight of swirling white-water rapids just a bit further down. No wonder the water pressure was quickening. My impulse was to reach out and grab him, but the voice said, "Wait until he comes up!" The powerful current was slamming against me and it took all of my strength and effort not to be swept downriver. Yet I didn't fear for my life at all. I felt strangely peaceful, knowing that I was deeply safe. I sensed I would survive being swept away, but that I would fail in my mission to save him if I lost my footing against the current. I knew in these split seconds that this was a karmic moment. It was my task to save him, a task I'd failed in a previous incarnation. All of this recognition, the voices telling me what to do, the panoramic scene—it all happened in seconds, yet it was crystal clear and very slow.

The moment his head bobbed up from within the vortex, I was able to grab his shoulder and pull him toward me and then toward the shore. Coughing and spluttering, he recovered on the sand. Looking up the river, we could no longer see our starting point. We had been drawn so far down and around a bend that our friends had no idea where we were and no one would have looked for us for a very long time. Spirit had saved his life, and guided me to fulfill a karmic contract.

I have found that people who were good communicators when alive often continue to be excellent at sending easily understood messages from the other side. Those who were known for their quiet countenance continue to express few words once they've crossed over. Clairaudience is a two-way street, with two beings talking to each other through an energetic system. Once the message has been sent to us, it is our responsibility to receive the transmission and interpret it. Over time, accuracy comes from both correct reception and correct interpretation of what we have received.

TELEPATHY

Telepathy is a part of clairvoyance but is often thought of as direct conversations between people or thought transference. It operates exactly the same way as clairaudient information from a Spirit guide, although we often turn the message around to be heard as a personal thought. We receive telepathic communication from our friends using the same receptor—the fifth chakra, in the throat. The information is translated in the base of the skull and often seems like we're just thinking, except those thoughts often seem to "come out of nowhere."

For example, if Brandon's boss is thinking, "Brandon isn't a good fit in this department but he's got potential. I should talk to HR and see about training and transfer possibilities."

Simultaneously, Brandon might think:

"I wonder if I'm going to get fired—it's strange, I think the boss likes me but lately I'm not so sure," or

"I should try to get more training and move to another department," or

"I need to get a new job—soon."

In the examples above, Brandon's mind responds to the telepathic message in various ways, from fear and confusion to an impulse to take action. To Brandon, the thoughts feel like his own.

The main point here is that most people don't hear a telepathic message exactly as the message is sent. The message is turned around as if it's your own thoughts. Life gets a whole lot easier as you learn to listen to telepathic messages and begin to trust that you're hearing the thoughts of other people. With time you can learn to identify messages from others versus your own fears and anxieties, and also perceive the message exactly. Then you may act on your intuition with clarity.

So in this example, Brandon could open the conversation with his boss: "You know I've been wondering if my skills are really a good fit for this department...?" Or he could decide he doesn't want to be transferred and begin a job search.

Sometimes the telepathic thoughts we receive keep changing. This usually means we're picking up on changing thoughts about something rather than a reception error.

Tara had plans for lunch with Becky on a Wednesday at noon. When Tara woke up she had an immediate feeling that Becky was going to cancel on her, yet as she finished her breakfast she found herself thinking, "She's going to be there." Around

10:30 she suddenly had the thought, "You should check with Becky and make sure she's not going to be late." Tara dismissed this thought, reminding herself that Becky was a Capricorn with a Virgo moon and she was always punctual. At 10:45, the feelings in Becky's gut were strong. She felt heavy and had a mild sense of foreboding. She *thought*, "call her now," but became distracted with email and forgot. At 11:45 Tara felt fine, began packing things up, and looked forward to the lunch.

When Becky arrived she told her what a hard morning she'd had. She woke up with an upset stomach and was thinking of canceling but after drinking some tea she felt better. Then her boss handed her a big project she wanted done by noon and she thought either she would have to cancel or she'd be late. She almost called mid-morning to cancel but then a co-worker offered to help with the assignment; it was completed on time and finally she was out the door. Tara's clear intuitive hits lined up with the play-by-play of what had actually happened.

If you sometimes think you're crazy
because of mixed messages,
you may be experiencing *actual* mixed messages.

A clear mind allows you to "hear" various clairaudient messages. They may come from your high Self, Spirit guides, friends or the animal world. Learning to trust this listening aspect of intuition enhances your ability to meet life as it shifts and changes.

SPIRIT GUIDES

Spirit guides are always guiding us, whether we are aware that these subtle conversations are happening in our minds or not. People often ask me if they have "any" Spirit guides. I'm also asked how to get Spirit guides to "come back" when they've left. Truth is, they haven't gone anywhere no matter how ungrateful, closed down or "bad" we think we are.

Some people think we have to ask our Spirit guides to help us. Their help is more direct and obvious when we ask, and also seems to be stronger when we thank them regularly, but they are there helping whether we ask or not. Endlessly loyal, they are there even if we're ungrateful.

We all have Spirit guides. They are a necessity—not optional. They don't actually ever go anywhere, because they exist in a plane of existence that allows them to be present everywhere at once, much as we imagine "God" or Spirit to be. It's just sometimes we feel their presence more viscerally or we hear their messages. The rest of the time they are in the background, working their magic.

Spirit is a diffuse energy permeating all of life. There are levels of separation within the wholeness. We can perceive the difference between one Spirit guide and another, or our own High Self from a Spirit guide, and yet from their point of view they are one energy, or attuned to the Oneness, the fabric of connection. This is especially true for the higher Spirit beings, the ones who have finished their earthly incarnations. They tell me they are One from their perspective, but they understand that we humans see them as individual spirits.

Does each drop of water in the ocean know it is separate?

Some people worry they have angered their guides by not doing what they want. True Spirit guides are your loving friends. They are here to help you realize your dreams, in alignment with your soul's path. They do not make decisions for you nor tell you what to do.

You can trust that you have Spirit guides, usually at least three and often ten or more. They can be people you have known who have crossed over, your children-to-be, souls you've known in other lives, or healing or teaching masters. You may have animals as guides. Animal guides can be a wide variety of real or magical animal Spirits available to all, or personal animals you have known as pets in this life. You can also call in guides for particular reasons, such as when you enter a new profession or are in need of specialized healing.

If you feel you have a spirit around you who is chastising, controlling or negative, that is not a true Spirit "guide." That is considered a spirit entity, ghost or demonic energy. As we explore connecting with your guides, we will carefully word what we say and do to invite in only the highest level Spirit guides.

Whether you are getting information from your own guides or getting a reading from someone else, it is always important that you listen to your own intuition by feeling for a sense of resonance in your body.

Guides won't give you information that allows you to avoid necessary painful experiences. This is significant. Your soul's path and your karma have priority. Unlike us, spirits don't make avoiding suffering a priority. They know you must experience life to awaken. If you need to travel down a rocky path to get there, they will hold you in Light and protect you from anything that isn't supposed to happen—that hasn't been chosen from the highest level of consciousness. But they won't help you avoid all suffering or prevent what *seems* like a mistake at the time.

ONE GUIDE AT A TIME

When you begin to connect with Spirit guides, get to know them well and develop a strong connection. Work with one guide at a time (or a couple of well-known beings) to ensure the process unfolds safely.

It's risky to talk to every spirit that shows up each time you go into meditation. Opening up to your psychic gifts can be fascinating and even addictive. I've seen people go to one class and be amazed at the accurate information they received. Soon all of their friends are asking for readings and each time there is a different guide who talks to them. Suddenly the information turns dark, negative, fear inducing, traumatic or dramatic—and just plain wrong. Verifying the guide was from the Light became "just too much work" and the students were enjoying the different experiences with a variety of spirits. Often, mediocre or even dark entities hang around psychic students just waiting for an opportunity to create a bit of havoc.

Negative spirits "feed" on dramatic, fearful, intense emotional energy and enjoy creating problems. High-level, positive spirits wish to create more peace and evolution. Their messages will be uplifting, empowering and helpful.

When you focus on getting to know the first high-level guide you have connected to, over time as you are ready you will be introduced or passed along to higher guides. This avoids the risks of receiving harmful information.

A BRIEF GUIDE TO GUIDES

Astral Guides: These guides are in between lives and offer personal details and assistance with your path. At least one main Spirit guide and several others will be of this type—your "friends" and soul family from life to life. Depending on their clarity they will help you achieve your highest soul's path, but their perspective might not be of the highest spiritual nature.

Ancestral Guides: All of us can enjoy and receive the help of family members, past and future. Like astral guides, these guides can be wonderful with details, but may have a family karma agenda. Mom still wants you to marry a nice man, until she's been in the Light long enough to dissolve some of her human thought patterns. The spirits who will be your children are often around you as guides until they are born. Loved ones and family members who pass to the other side are also astral guides, even if you never met them. They can provide great details and powerful worldly help when they've been alive on Earth recently.

Extraterrestrials: ET beings from the Pleiades, Orion and other dimensions are helping Earth at this time. Beware of less evolved ETs. Even the higher level ETs may have a personal agenda behind the information they give.

Healing/Teaching Masters and Ascended Masters: These guides often have the highest spiritual wisdom but will not usually offer detailed personal direction. Their wisdom often resonates very deeply within us on a heart level.

Archangels: A group of very high beings, available to all. Archangel Michael is especially important to us in helping clear dark entities and spirits from our world.

Angels: A special class of spirits who do not generally take physical incarnation. They provide nurturing, support, comfort, and healing and bring us into connection with Higher Self.

Jesus, Buddha, Quan Yin, Tara, Mother Mary and other well-known Beings from various belief systems: These loving high Beings are available to all of us, so don't be surprised if one of these masters come to you in a Spirit guide meditation. You actually *are* special enough to deserve this kind of guide. Shiva, Sita and Ram, Lakshmi, Hanuman, and various other Hindu deities may also be your guides, whether you think of them as separate or as divine qualities within.

Spirit Animals: Spirit animals have a long history in indigenous and ancient cultures. You are likely to be aligned with one animal and may have many others, especially as you develop or need the qualities embodied by a particular animal.

When an animal spirit makes contact with you, it might come into your dreams, or you might have a direct experience unexpectedly in real life. Feel the message or protection they bring you. Once you begin to connect with the Spirit realm deliberately through meditation, your Spirit animals will show up more clearly. Cultivate your relationship with each one.

Here are some of the general qualities of various animals, reptiles, insects and birds with which you can align when you connect with their spirit. Imagine you *are* the animal, rather than imagining them as a separate being guiding you.

Alligators & Crocodiles: Primal energies, protection, survival, risk, revenge

Bear: Introspection, psychic ability within/through hibernation, strength & protection, mother bear, power, wisdom

Beaver: collaboration, cooperation, building/working toward goals

Birds in general: messengers, freedom

Buffalo: good fortune, healing, strength, stability

Butterfly: transformation, joy, evolution, light

Caribou: abundance, rebirth

Cat: sensuality, peacefulness, independence, mystery

Coyote: trickster teacher, karmic situations, intelligence

Crow: assertiveness, knowledge of spiritual laws, message to pay attention, shapeshifter

Deer: gentleness, grace, heart, sensitivity

Dog: loyalty, courage, unconditional love

Dolphin: playfulness, connection to Spirit, happiness

Dove: peace, love, gentleness

Dragons: power, transformation, magic (a form of snake), longevity

Dragonfly: illusions, dreams, hypnotherapy, traveling through the veils

Eagle: freedom, teaching and leadership power, clear vision

Elephant: wisdom, strength, prosperity, abundance

Fox: adaptable, clever, intelligence, cunning

Frog: cleansing, feminine energy, creation

Giraffe: seeing the higher aspects, discrimination, elegance

Goat: tenacity, mischief, virility

Grasshopper: abundance, prosperity

Hawk: Attention to detail, vision, spirituality, messenger

Horse: power, freedom, stamina, nobility

Hummingbird: joy, messenger, vitality

Leopard: strength, stealth

Lion: strength, courage, authority

Lizard: dreaming, vision
Moose: strength, accomplishment, self-esteem
Mountain Lion: Strength, agility
Mouse: attention to detail
Otter: playfulness, sensuality, female power
Owl: magic, omens, wisdom, vision
Phoenix: transformation, rising out of difficult circumstances
Porcupine: self-protection
Puma: power, desire, grace
Rabbit: fear, and confronting fears mindfully, vigilance
Ram: new beginnings, growth
Raccoon: disguise and cleverness, ingenuity, manual dexterity
Red hawk: insight, truth
Skunk: reputation, walk your talk, presence
Snake: transmutation, rebirth, power, wisdom
Tiger: courage, sexuality, power
Turtle: Mother Earth, home, protective, longevity, navigation
Vulture: purification, vision, renewal
Wolf: teacher, loyalty, loner

3. Clairvoyance

Clairvoyance is the ability to see energy—"clear seeing." This subtle visual skill allows you to see auras and chakras, visions of past lives and probable realities in the future. You can also view the inside of the body (medical intuition), see the nature of relationships between people, or see symbolic information about current situations. Any psychic picture that comes to you intuitively via the third eye is called clairvoyance.

The third eye is the sixth chakra in the center of the forehead, or some would say, "between the eyebrows." One sign that you have natural visual abilities is that your dreams are clear, although you might not remember your dreams if you're tired or stressed. Another clue to your natural seeing skill is if you are

a visual learner. You might notice that when people are talking, you imagine a picture of what they're talking about in your mind spontaneously. These pictures are subtle and soft, sometimes fleeting. Even if you think you don't see psychic pictures easily, you can develop this ability with meditation and practice.

When this ability is more challenged, it might be because you "saw" too much, as children or in prior lives. Often the rejection or punishment for being a "seer" was severe. Closing down the vision of the third eye might have been a survival skill at one point.

It is easiest to see clairvoyantly with eyes closed and in a moderately dim room. Too much light coming into your eyes through your eyelids will make it difficult to see the images in your mind's eye. If you have your eyes open, the brain processes the physical visual images strongly. Clairvoyants who "see" with eyes open either cast their eyes upward or downward to dim the vision of material reality.

If you close your eyes so that your physical visual sight is restricted, you will see more details clairvoyantly. In fact, as you close your eyes and focus on different questions, or intend to see into different areas of the aura, a stream of information can be received.

When you see psychically, the possibilities are multidimensional. You might see the emotional energy, an old karmic wound, or the organ energy inside of the body. This can be confusing initially, because the first answer you receive via a picture then turns into another picture. As you continue to focus, yet another picture arises. Which is the correct one? The answer is they are all correct, perhaps in a sequence, or perhaps answering different aspects of the same question. There is a risk that your mind will reject the first answer and make up a more palatable answer. As you practice, you will learn to simply allow images to arise without judgment.

There are various chakra systems. Let's embrace diversity even here. It's energy. It's not like a table that can be measured and described in a somewhat similar fashion by different viewers. And although I understand the mental desire to integrate various systems, it usually doesn't work well to attempt to integrate other metaphysical systems with the chakras. Some will match well and others won't. The interpretations become less crisp. There will be ways in which systems intersect and ways in which they differ. Energy is changeable; it flows and morphs. And it responds to thought. Whatever system you're working with will work for you. Most modern metaphysical practitioners use a basic seven chakra system with some level of consistency about what each chakra means. There are also higher spiritual chakras and hand and foot chakras to consider if you wish to go deeper. We'll keep it simple with a seven chakra system for this discussion.

This table shows each chakra and its associated gland, as well as its name and qualities. The colors are colors that heal or resonate with this chakra. If you look at an aura clairvoyantly, most of the time the chakras are not the color you might imagine from looking at chakra paintings and diagrams, which show us "ideal" versions of chakras. They can be many colors, or, honestly are often dim, dark or hard to see.

You will see in the chart under "Other attributes of the color . . ." that some colors match the chakra qualities and some are completely different. I'm not willing to make color healing philosophies that work in real life match chakra qualities. It's interesting to explore the colors you're drawn to as they relate to chakras or qualities of life you're repelled by or attracted to.

Chakra (gland in that area)	Name	Main Purpose	Qualities of Chakra	Color that resonates or heals this chakra	Other attributes of the color might be:
First (adrenal)	Root	Survival	Survival level sexuality, grounding, physical health, security	Red	Vitality, anger, rage, life force, passion, courage, temper, ambition, sexual, materialism, sport
Second (ovaries/ testes)	Sacral	Emotions	Emotionally based Sexuality, creativity, strong emotion, rage, anger, connection	Orange	Warm-hearted, healing, social, connection to external world,
Third (pancreas)	Power/ Solar Plexus	Power	Control, manipulation, self-esteem, self-worth, manifestation	Yellow	Well-being, social, fear or anxiety, intellect, creativity, talkative

Chakra (gland in that area)	Name	Main Purpose	Qualities of Chakra	Color that resonates or heals this chakra	Other attributes of the color might be:
Fourth (thymus)	Heart	Love	Joy, grief, sadness, betrayal	Green or pink	Green is new growth, healing, love to others, money, prosperity, fertility, love of nature, Pink is more self-love, nurturing, giving
Fifth (thyroid)	Throat	Communication	Expression, creativity	Blue	People oriented, inner peace, cooling & calming, serenity, creative, talkative, writing
Sixth (pineal)	Third Eye	Vision	Mental, Clairvoyance, Intuition, Devotion	Indigo	Psychic, visionary

Chakra (gland in that area)	Name	Main Purpose	Qualities of Chakra	Color that resonates or heals this chakra	Other attributes of the color might be:
Seventh (pituitary)	Crown	Spiritual/Source	Channeling, Knowing, Awareness, Oneness with God	Purple/ Violet, Gold, White	Purple: power, higher spiritual development White: truth, purity, cleansing, protection Gold: Service to others, powerful spiritual color, protective, wealth, baby might be coming if found in womb
				Brown	Practicality, material success, perhaps depression, Groundedness, nature connection, boring
				Black	Unconscious, mysterious, deep depression, evil, protection, blockage

A Note About Dreams

Dreams can be an important source of healing and information and are connected to the sixth chakra.

Precognitive dreams foretell the future

Astral Contact Dreams are actual connections and conversations with both living people and spirits from the other side.

Past-Life Dreams often take place in a different historical period and are

Repetitive.

General Process Dreams are the most common.

PRECOGNITIVE DREAMS

A precognitive dream foretells the future. Sometimes they are very simple and direct, such as a dream where you hear a voice that tells you a fact: You will receive a promotion. The green chair will break.

A precognitive dream may also be longer, like little vignettes, with a story that unfolds.

In a precognitive dream, Melissa was planning to buy a house with her husband. Her sister was going to finance the down payment for them. As Melissa worked with realtors to find the right house, she dreamed:

I was standing on a hill overlooking a panorama of hills, highways and roads, a vast vista. A car drove up to the top of the hill and my sister got out, looking more like a banker than her normal self. She said, "I'm not going to give you the money for the down payment, I'm sorry." When I asked why, she pointed toward the freeway. There were two huge semi-trucks driving side by side down the freeway. All of a sudden they stopped and collapsed into a rubbery mess.

When she woke up the next morning, she didn't understand what the dream meant but was concerned about the down payment money. She called her sister to find out if everything was still on track. Her sister told her that actually, no, she had decided that her marriage wasn't strong enough and she didn't want to risk lending them the down payment money. She didn't feel they should buy a house at this time.

The two huge semi-trucks represented Melissa and her husband going down the path (freeway) but suddenly stopping and collapsing (divorce, the relationship dissolves). They unexpectedly decided to divorce a few months later.

ASTRAL CONTACT DREAMS

Astral contact dreams are very clear dreams of a connection with another person or spirit. In these dreams it can seem like you are "sitting" across from someone. You might see the upper part of the other person as if you are both floating in space. There might be little or no communication, or a very active communication.

Astral contact dreams are often precognitive, foretelling the future.

Frances had a dream that she was sitting with her good friend Sarah. They were simply floating in space, looking at each other. Sarah said, "I'm going to have a baby" very calmly and with a big smile. A few days later she took a pregnancy test and called to tell Frances the news.

PAST-LIFE DREAMS

Past-life dreams are historic in nature and are often repetitive, and seem to occur more when you are young.

One person dreamed of being in a ditch, the sounds of battle all around him. Another dreamed of being in a beautiful dress, dancing with a handsome man in the center of a room that was clearly seventeenth century. A past-life regression or meditation to experience this dream fully will help to resolve it so the dreams will end.

GENERAL PROCESS DREAMS

Most dreams fall under this category. The mind is categorizing and processing the day's events. We need abundant sleep to accomplish all of this processing and wake up clear and refreshed.

Many of us have been sleep-deprived for years—or decades. We are exhausted, tired in body and spirit. It's a gift to our dream processing futures that current research supports the need for more sleep (7 to 12 hours per night depending on age). Perhaps we will create balanced sleep patterns to be able to process all that we need to transform while sleeping.

HOW TO ANALYZE OR RESOLVE DREAMS

If you don't remember dreams or don't dream very often, try to get more sleep. This helps a lot. Sometimes it helps to sleep long enough that you can wake up without an alarm clock. Other times an interruption in the middle of the night or the alarm will be what wakes you right in the middle of vivid dreaming. Either way, try not to move physically as you remember the dream. If you sat up, return to the same position you were in while dreaming. This too helps with recall. Once you've remembered the dream, write down whatever you can recall.

To analyze dreams when the meaning is not immediately clear, write the dream down double-spaced. Then review the written dream and for every noun or object word, think of a brief generic description of that thing as if you were explaining it to a newcomer to the planet. Look up symbolic meanings if you wish as well.

If the dream is in the kitchen, you might find a symbol interpretation that a kitchen is a place of nurturing. Or you could say, "I was in the part of a living structure where nourishing food is cooked."

Some people say that every person in a dream is a reflection of you, or a part of you, so if your mom is in the dream you are seeing the motherly part of yourself. You can analyze your dreams in this way, to see every single thing meaning you or a part of you. This works because from a spiritual perspective, we are all one and everyone we know is a projection. But it is also true that all of the aspects of ourselves show up in the physical reality as other people and as objects. You may well be getting a message that someone you know is going to do something. Your mom may do or say whatever you saw in the dream. It can be beneficial to analyze dreams from both perspectives.

From a spiritual perspective, everything you dream is about you because of the core principle of oneness. If you can hold that truth as the container, you can still interpret your dreams, unfold the precognitive nature and also appreciate the astral contact with friends and family.

For a deeper exploration of dreams, see the work of Greg Bogart in the Bibliography.

4. Channeling

Channeling is the intuitive process of bringing information, creativity or healing energy from a high-level spiritual source directly through you via the crown, or seventh chakra. The high-level spiritual source might be a Spirit guide or your own Higher Self. Or it could come from vast energies of awareness, creativity, imagination and healing that are available to all.

When you channel information spontaneously, it will feel like a sudden "knowingness"—like an inner bolt of lightning. There is a pure and simple feel to this awareness; it's not usually caught up with words and complexities. It's more like a feeling of knowing truth without doubt.

Although this deep sense of inner knowing may be very clear, many people have a challenging time trusting this flow of guidance because it's harder to pinpoint where it came from. You don't see a picture in your mind. You don't hear a voice. You just know.

If this is a strong intuitive gift for you, use visual meditation to open your crown chakra to the correct level of openness for you. If it is too open, you might draw in a huge flow of information so the higher messages become diluted and the information floods in without a discernible stream. If it is closed or narrowed, you will feel cut off from source and your inner knowing.

Allow one high Spirit being you can trust to be your main channeling connection. When you evolve yourself to the point you are ready to channel another guide, your main guide will introduce the new one to you.

Protect your head and crown chakra by wearing a hat or scarf when outdoors, especially if you're in a crowded place. This will feel comforting if you are an extra-sensitive person via the crown chakra.

REFLECTION #11

1. Meditation #11.1: Run Energy, Ground and Create Boundaries

Running Energy: Begin by placing your body in a comfortable position. Breathe deeply and slowly.

Draw your attention from the heart area up through the center of your head, imagining you are tethered to a fine silvery cord attached deep just below the heart chakra area, near the solar plexus. From this cord, you are going up through the roof if you're in a building, overlooking the trees, moving toward the clouds, drawn to and through the stars, and arriving at a huge golden globe of Universal Energy.

Enter this place and notice the many available swirling colors. Choose a color or colors that appeal to you and draw them back down your cord, swirling the energy in a spiral around your cord. Draw this color down through the central core of your body, along the spine, dropping out the base of the tailbone/pelvic area where you will see or imagine a thick grounding rope that goes deep into the earth. Continue to draw your chosen color of cosmic energy down the cord into the Earth, passing rocks, water and layers of Earth crust.

At the center of the Earth imagine a huge circle of swirling colors. Breathe into this core earth energy; choose a color or colors to bring up the cord. Draw these colors up your cord, through the central core of your body, and then release them through the crown of your head, some going straight up to the stars, some perhaps bubbling like a fountain over your body.

Now breathe into your heart and mix the two streams of color. With each inhale imagine the colors are spreading into your physical body. When the physical body is dense with Light, allow the colored Light to expand into the aura, a huge oval shape that is three feet all the way around you, over your head, under your feet, paying attention to your back and sides as well as the front of your body.

Boundaries. When you are completely filled up, imagine a boundary of beautiful sparkly Light all the way around your aura. This Light may be gold, silver, purple, indigo or some other bright clear color. If you need a stronger boundary, imagine it to be metal like a shield, or particularly thick. Play with the boundary colors and materials until you find the right boundary for different situations in your life. With close friends, an inch-thick sparkly purple might be perfect. For a visit to a busy place like a vibrant restaurant, a shopping mall or rock concert, you might want several layers of Light, including the sparkly layer closest in to you, then metal (like King Arthur's shields) and perhaps thick white Light as well. Be aware that your psychic receptors will feel a bit shut down with this much protection and you might feel a bit dull. When you return from the event, remove the extra layers and get comfortable with a lighter protection.

2. Meditation #11.2: Chakra Balance

Once you are comfortable with the meditation to run energy, visualize each chakra one by one, beginning with the first at the base of the spine and moving up through each one.

- *Breathe into each chakra and simply imagine it opening up.*

- *Visualize the vortex shape of the chakra from narrow at its beginning near the spine and gradually increasing in size like a large ice cream cone.*
- *Visualize a color of light swirling through it.*
- *Visualize the violet/purple flame burning through it and then filling the empty space with a color of light.*
- *Swirl all chakras in a clockwise or counterclockwise direction, as long as they are going the same way.*

3. Meditation #11.3: Spirit Guide Connection

Breathe deeply and imagine you are outside in nature. Invite your highest-level Spirit guide to show up. If this is your familiar guide and you are sure they are of the Light, continue. Otherwise ask these two clarifying questions:

1.   Are you of the Light?
2.   Are you the highest guide available to me now?

If they say yes or you are filled with a loving sense of presence, continue on.

If they say no or disappear, ask for the true Light guide to show up.

Once you are sure your highest guide is with you, if they are new to you, ask:

1.   How long have you been with me?
2.   What is your role in my life?
3.   Do you have a message for me?

Once you have met with the guide more than once, you can always ask for a message or ask questions.

4. Meditation #11.4: Pink & Green Meditation

In this variation of Meditation #11.1 - Grounding and Running Energy, choose pink and green light and run them through your whole body, mixing them at the heart. Weave the energy back and forth from left to right and back again, like an infinity symbol, a figure eight on its side.

Find a balance that feels comfortable to you intuitively so you have a solid base of pink light in your heart and in your aura to reflect self-love and self-acceptance, and you also have a reasonable level of green light in your heart and aura to reflect your devotion and love to others.

This will be a different balance for each person, and different perhaps from time to time in life.

5. Journal Reflection: Clairsentience & Empathy. *To practice feeling skills, this classic psychometry exercise can be illuminating. Find an object that belongs to someone you don't know too well. It can be a piece of jewelry or keys or an article of clothing they wear often. Hold the object in your left hand and allow the energy of the person to come to you through the object. Notice if the object feels cool or warm, and allow a list of words that describe the person to come to your mind. Ask if there's a message for the person. Write down what you get. (P.S.: give the object back.)*

Rebuild the Aura: If you think you might be extra-sensitive to energy and your left side may be frayed, after you've done a meditation to run energy from cosmos and Earth into your aura, spend extra time padding the left side of your body and your aura with this colored light. Visualize the boundary to be extra strong and thick.

6. Journal Reflection: Clairaudience & Telepathy
Connect with a Spirit Guide: After your calming meditation, connect with your Spirit guide. This can be part of Meditation #11.3 or if you feel a strong connection with your guide, simply as you sit, at the end of the meditation,

ask for a message and write it down. The message can be general, or about an issue, or advice for the day.

Telepathy with a Friend: For telepathy with another person, practice sending strong thoughts to people you know. Think of the person and imagine you are saying something simple and direct to them, like, "Please bring me a coconut water," or "I love your hair." Notice whatever validation you receive that people are hearing you.

7. Journal Reflection: Clairvoyance & Vision

Close your eyes and imagine a person you know is standing in front of you. Allow the screen in your mind to see the colors of their energy field. You can scan the inner image from the top to the bottom. Draw a picture of what you've received.

8. Journal Reflection: Channeling

Automatic writing is an "old school" psychic skill that can be an excellent tool to develop channeling and spirit connection, especially if you're feeling challenged by visual or direct communication. Some spirits are particularly good at transmitting this way, and this might be an easier way for you to get past any resistance you have. Plus, you have a written record of your conversation and the advice you received.

1. Prepare by getting a pad of paper or journal and a pen, or having your computer or tablet set to a text/word processing app. You can also use a recording app and speak rather than write.

2. Center yourself by meditating for at least a few minutes, preferably five to ten or more, to calm your mind and reduce the thinking process.

3. Think about the Spirit guide or departed loved one you'd like to contact, saying their name in your mind over and over.

4. Start writing (or recording) whatever words, thoughts or phrases come into your mind. Describe any pictures that flash into your mind. At first the words coming through might seem a bit stilted or slow. There's a tendency to say to yourself that you're "making it up." Continue anyway, ignoring these distracting thoughts. Let yourself relax into a stream of consciousness mode in which you record as fast as you can write or type. As you become comfortable with this process, you can ask specific questions by saying them in your mind or writing them down, and then going back to the stream of consciousness writing.

5. Then, and this is important, DO NOT READ what you have written. Put it away for at least three days, preferably a week or longer. This is how long it will take for the memory of the words moving through your brain to fade.

6. When the waiting time has passed, read your message. Most people are surprised by what they have transcribed, as it doesn't seem like it is something they would have known or written themselves.

CHAPTER TWELVE

The Mental Pillar

"Why sometimes I've believed as many as six
impossible things before breakfast."
—from Lewis Carroll's Alice in Wonderland

How do you talk to yourself? If you could listen to a recorded version of your unconscious mental chatter while you go through your day, you'd be shocked. If anyone else talked to you that way you would end the relationship. Endless suggestions, criticisms, questions . . . Nag would be a serious understatement.

Even when you've been meditating and clearing the mind for some time, events can trigger a resurgence of the thought patterns you "thought" you got rid of a long time ago.

We can't have a discussion about thought without talking about the power of positive thinking. This theory of how to create a better life has gained significant attention over the past forty years. You might have even tried to change your life by changing your thoughts. *I am wealthy, thin and beautiful! I am wealthy, thin and beautiful . . .*

Are we there yet?

Positive thought is one of those theoretically correct truths that is a lot harder and more nuanced than it seems on the surface. It makes sense, but usually the resistance of the old thoughts are so strong that positive thoughts just seem to excite the negative thoughts to try harder. It takes so long to create change we give up. Much of what we're manifesting in this moment is based on thoughts we had years ago, so even daily positive thought marathons can take time to create effective change. And, sometimes we attain a goal and feel it's not even the right one. Success feels flat.

In this section we begin the exploration of the mind, and particularly the mental part of the mind. There is a difference between the human personal thinking mind and the spiritual concept of "Mind" just as there is a distinction between our self in an ego/personality way and Self that might be called "High Self."

Creation and manifestation of your physical life originated from this high "Mind," the intentional vibration of the soul. Then as you manifest into physical incarnation (as in, you're born as a baby) you have a human mind that now has its own thought agenda to add to the mix. The thoughts are based on past-life memories manifested within the aura and embryo imprinting— that karmic layer of clothes on top of your beautiful spirit Self.

Human level thoughts are intertwined with emotions. Each leads to the other. You can easily test this. If you deliberately think about something sad—for instance worrying that someone you love will die—you will immediately feel sadness as if it is true and already happening. Your brain can't actually tell the difference between a real event and your imagination of it and you respond emotionally to your thoughts whether they are true or not. And conversely, if you're having a sad, discouraging day for no apparent reason, you will think of various reasons to justify your feelings. You'll be looking at the glass half full, fearful or anxious about possible undesirable events.

We will now contemplate thought as a separate issue; emotional healing will follow in the next section.

Thoughts Create Reality

Thoughts create reality. Or, as Mike Dooley of the famed *Notes from the Universe* says: "thoughts become things." What kind of things, you might say?

You will create exactly what you're thinking over time, laid on top of the soul path you were originally born with, which was created from higher Mind.

The soul path was the blueprint. The thoughts are the gasoline you're pouring in the engine of creation to manifest the intention.

If your thoughts are random and contradictory, guess what? Your life will move up and down, sideways and in circles.

If your thoughts are clear and organized, relatively positive and focused, *and in alignment with the original blueprint,* you will move toward your goals with much more ease.

The problem with most people's minds is they tend to operate like a continual random thought-generating machine. From morning until night, seven days a week, the mind talks endlessly. You can find yourself thinking a stream of erratic thoughts that have very little to do with who you are, what is true for you, or what you actually wish to create.

The unexamined mind is like a recording device that has recorded everything you've ever heard from the time you were in your mother's belly all the way to this point in time. You might not even be consciously aware of what you've heard. It could have been the dialogue of television shows and commercials, or the radio blaring in the background. Your mind remembers mean taunts from other children at school and bits and pieces from your parents arguing in another room. This powerful and detailed recording device also remembers and plays back the thoughts you've picked up from other people telepathically underneath their well-meaning (but not necessarily honest) words.

The recorded information has also been filtered through your personal mind interpreter, which can be understood by looking at your astrological makeup. Are you likely to be positive and hopeful? Do you see life as a series of challenges and ulterior motives? Rose-colored glasses, or dark shields?

Your thought patterns will be amplified by your emotional nature and the backlog of feelings you carry that have not been processed. This combination of unprocessed feelings and mental constructs form your "hot buttons" or triggers, the patterns that create whatever reality you experience.

Unless you have done a significant amount of mental healing, all of these words or pictures that have been recorded will play back on an endless loop—white noise in the background. Most of us don't even notice everything we're thinking. Then when a life situation comes up, the mind instantaneously researches that subject in the mental library and the recording plays, regurgitating a series of comments.

Unless you have woken up to this automatic system and done something to tame the mind, you will believe that these thoughts automatically playing back are "me" and "mine" and will speak and act from this perspective.

As humans we are conditioned to believe "if I think this, it must be who I am." We tell others, "I always do this" and "I believe this" or "I know this"—yet often we haven't examined where we got it from, how we know it, or if it is actually true for us. Without specific attention to how or why, you have decided you are made up of a variety of characteristics that might include smart, driven, lazy, hopeless or . . . lucky or unlucky.

The problem isn't so much *that* we think, because we will always have a mind and be subject to thought process. The problem is that we *identify* with the thoughts. We actually believe thought. We think thought is us. And it is not. I repeat: you are not your thoughts. Your thoughts happen by themselves based on all of this programming.

Now, this story isn't a statistical study, but I found it interesting and believable. Reported in *The Luck Factor* by Richard Wiseman, a researcher filmed two people, Martin and Brenda. They had volunteered to participate in a research study, but didn't know what the study was about. In the preliminary interview intake, Brenda said she was "unlucky" and Richard said he was definitely "very lucky." They were told to meet a researcher at a cafe to find out more about the project.

A five-dollar bill was left on the ground in front of the cafe. As he walked to the cafe to meet the researcher, Martin saw the bill, picked it up, went in and sat at the counter and talked to a businessman (who was actually the researcher). Brenda walked the same path to the cafe (where they had again laid a five-dollar bill in the same place), didn't see the bill, sat down at the counter but didn't talk to the businessman/researcher who was still there.

After the experiment was over, the researchers interviewed them both, asking them specifically if they thought anything lucky or unlucky had happened during their day. Martin was excited about finding the money and the nice conversation he'd had with an interesting guy at the counter; Brenda described her day as uneventful.

Both of them had the same opportunity; only one of them seized the opportunity.

You can probably remember many times in life when you've been in a bad mood and went through the day feeling isolated and alone, not talking to anyone, and other times when you felt upbeat and friendly and had various positive interactions with other people. It simply makes sense we will have better experiences when we feel better. Current brain research affirms this through study after study. When we believe we are likely to have positive experiences, we actually do have more positive experiences. It's statistical.

Whether you have occasional or many negative thoughts about yourself and your life, it makes sense to spend some healing focus on changing these words and patterns to more positive ideas.

There is, however, a downside to this intentional positivity.

The ultimate goal of spiritual awakening is to be able to meet life as it arises, without judging whether life is good or bad, positive or negative. We experience true freedom when we are unattached to the outcome.

Just as the meditations to practice different types of intuitive skills cultivate a pathway to be connected to our natural intuition throughout the day, positive thinking is a temporal healing technique to help us clear habituated negative thoughts so we can ultimately learn to be present with reality as it is. Positive thinking is a reasonable antidote to negative thinking. It stops endless negative patterns that are unnecessarily creating a negative reality. Once we have come to some level of balance, or perhaps while we're coming to balance, we can take the next steps to learn to accept life with equanimity.

Mental healing is a process to quiet the mind, to undo negative recorded programming and to learn to be with our experiences in the moment. As we do this, we can hear our heart and the messages of the soul. We begin to feel true, in-the-moment feelings, hear the voice of intuition, and find a deeper connection with Spirit.

As mental healing processes create a clearer mental view, the appropriate use of the mind unfolds. The mind is empowered to carry out tasks, learn necessary skills, organize day-to-day existence, and to communicate clearly from a place of heart and soul.

The Cure: A Three Step Process

1. ZEN MEDITATION

The first step is Zen-style meditation. Meditation is the same recommendation for developing spiritually—and for increasing intuition. Zen is particularly effective for bringing awareness to how thought plays endlessly.

The Zen counting meditation is described in detail in the reflection section. You will count to ten with the breath. Whenever you find yourself thinking, you simply return to counting, starting back at one. This will show you how quickly or slowly your mind goes into automatic thinking.

2. THOUGHT MINDFULNESS

The second step is to be more mindful about your thoughts and words in daily life. This requires diligence and awareness, activating the inner observer, and watching without judgment. The task is to see and reduce negative habitual thoughts and words. If you don't know what you do, there is no way to change or soften the patterns.

What are your "habit words?" These are words you use constantly that have no real meaning, such as "like," "um," "really," "can't," "always," and "never." You can let some of them go and replace others with words and phrases that are actually true. For instance, instead of saying "can't" you learn to say "choose not to."

What are you saying that is manifesting something you don't want?

Here's a perfect example of creating what you don't want through unexamined thought: Marta was partially supporting her brother and his family because she made a lot more money in her consulting business than they did in their jobs. Every month she gave them $500, appearing to be happy to be able to do it, but in her mind, she kept telling herself, "I can't afford to keep doing this." She would think, "They should try harder to make more money," feeling resentful while pretending to be perfectly fine with the arrangement. Month after month she found herself a little bit short in her own cash flow. She always had enough to pay her basic expenses, but with mindful attention to her thought process and to her budget, she realized she was telling herself over and over she couldn't afford to give them the $500, even though she did give it—and she was short about $500 every month to spend on extras she wanted. Her resentment arose because she was not able to take a weekend vacation or go to workshops that interested her. When she realized that her statement, "I can't afford to keep doing this," formed a negative belief that limited her income, she stopped herself whenever she had that thought and replaced it with, "I love to have enough money to do whatever I want and be able to help my family." Within two months her income increased to cover her gift to the family in addition to her desired expenditures.

Are you judging?

Notice when you are judging things in life as good or bad, including the thoughts you are now monitoring. Judgment solidifies energy. The mind loves to divide things up, good and bad, what I want, what I don't want. In this transitional healing period, you are noticing unconscious thoughts and changing them to more productive thoughts that will create a different outcome. That's true. However, a judgmental attitude will strengthen the negative thoughts.

As you review your thought habits, find a balance between softening around thoughts and making changes. A light and humorous touch is best.

3. POSITIVE THINKING

The third step is focused positive thinking. You can train yourself to think more positively. Notice your negative thoughts and erase them by saying the opposite positive thought at least three times. I think of the first positive thought only erasing the most recent one negative thought. Two or more positive thoughts begin to erase previous editions of that negative thought. You might have to say the positive thought a thousand times to erase the backlog, but over time you can cultivate the positive as automatically as thinking negative thoughts.

You are likely to have resistance to positive thinking in the beginning from inner parts who believe and hold the negative thoughts. These inner parts are connected to our emotional selves and will sabotage even the best mental reprogramming. They cannot be ignored. We will go into this in more detail in the next chapter on emotional healing and in Chapter 15. For now, simply find one recurring negative thought you have and formulate the countering positive thought.

For example, "I will never have . . ." (name a goal, thing or quality) becomes

"I have . . ." (goal, thing, quality). Simple, positive and present tense works the best.

Summary

Softly listen to your thinking with discernment but not judgment. Thoughts are a part of creating reality and a first step in clarifying the mind and intentions. We will fully explore in future sections the deeper and more complex aspects of how thoughts work in tandem with soul purpose, emotions and action.

You will come to understand that your thoughts are not actually "you" and that your thoughts are comprised of various random untruths. It is a good idea to reduce or reprogram these thought forms to create a different perspective of yourself and your reality—and to get a little mental rest.

The goal is ultimately to live with a quieter mind that is in alignment with soul path so that you understand and accept that life is unfolding perfectly. When you accurately see the way your mind works and substitute positive thoughts and beliefs for negative ones, you are healing erroneous patterns that don't actually reflect the spirit within.

And, one last thing: As you clear your mind of unnecessary chatter, you will be able to tell the difference between your own random thoughts and the words of intuition that come from inner spirit and knowingness, or the words of Spirit guides assisting you on your path.

#12 - REFLECTION

1. Meditation #12.1: Zen

Set your timer for five or ten minutes to start. Ultimately you might sit for thirty to sixty minutes, or even for hours as is common in meditation retreats.

Sit comfortably with your spine straight. You can choose to close your eyes partially, looking down a few feet in front of you, or position yourself so you are looking at a bare wall, yet still without strong attention to the wall.

You may sit cross-legged if that is comfortable for you. A "zafu" is a meditation cushion. You can sit on a zafu or another small pillow or rolled-up blanket to elevate your hips. If possible, let your knees touch the ground, allowing your sitting bones and knees to provide a stable, rooted base. Breathe into your sitting bones and rock the pelvis back and forth a little until you feel a firm foundation. You may also sit in a chair with spine straight and feet flat on the floor to ground your feet (without shoes). A small cushion behind your low back or a pillow under your feet is sometimes necessary for straight, easeful posture. *If your body cannot sit comfortably for even five or ten minutes, lie down.*

Place your hands in your lap, your left hand softly underneath your right if you are right-handed (right hand under the left if you are left-handed). Thumbs touch lightly.

Count to ten as you breathe. Inhale is one; exhale is two. Next inhale is three, exhale after that is four, and so on. Whenever you notice you have started to think, release the thought and then simply return to counting, beginning with one again. Do not resist or judge the thoughts, just release softly and restart the count. If you get to ten, begin at one again with the next breath.

You will begin to notice how the mind tends toward automatic thinking, returning back to the count of one, again and again. Perhaps you can be with the breath and experience each moment without judgment. You will notice that as soon as you feel you have "accomplished" success in breathing to ten that suddenly your mind kicks in and congratulates yourself and now you have a story and an engaged mind. It is so very tricky. Continuing to breathe in this way without judging whether you are doing it well or not well is the goal, which is then softened to no goal at all.

Once you can do this without much effort, the whole breath cycle of inhale and exhale can be counted as one, and the next inhale and exhale will be two. And so on.

2. Soul Path Offering: Thought Mindfulness & Positive Thinking

1. Be more mindful about your thoughts and words in daily life.
2. Notice habitual meaningless or negative words and speak more slowly so you are less inclined to use them.
3. Systematically replace habit words and phrases with words you believe are truer for you.
4. Notice your inclination to judge things as good or bad. See if you can breathe into being with whatever is happening without judgment.
5. When you notice a negative thought, think of an opposite positive thought and say it three times or more.
6. Laugh at yourself. Be light, loving and accepting of your humanness.

3. Journal Reflection: Your Thoughts and Beliefs as they relate to your Mission and Goals

Look at your Mission Statement and subgoals. What beliefs or thoughts do you have about your goals that are strong and helpful, negative or blocking? You might not know all of them at first. Allow the truth of your beliefs to emerge. If you've had a goal for some time and it hasn't manifested yet, consider what subconscious, blocking belief could be holding you back.

CHAPTER THIRTEEN

The Emotional Pillar

*"Healing comes from letting there be
room for all of 'this' to happen:
room for grief, for relief, for misery, for joy."*
—Pema Chödron

Emotion is like bacon and eggs. It used to be that you could eat them every day for a good hearty breakfast. Then "they" decided America's favorite breakfast was poison. Eggs had cholesterol and bacon was filled with the wrong kind of fat. Then another "they" started publishing articles saying sorry, we were wrong about that, just one (obviously mean-spirited) scientist with a bad study. And now, voila! . . . actually, eating cholesterol has nothing to do with blood cholesterol, which maybe has nothing to do with heart disease—maybe, maybe not—and to confuse us even more, suddenly, saturated fat isn't the problem. In fact, there's new evidence that eating more fat and less rice—innocuous, innocent rice—is beneficial for your health.

You can get to be so confused you just want to eat steamed veggies, which everyone agrees are a-okay (as of this writing).

Psychologists want us to feel our feelings, in depth, in order to release them. Freud suggested you had to get to the very bottom of them before building a new structure. Some spiritual traditions promote deepening a spiritual practice to learn to move beyond feelings. To them, feelings are negative, part of the ego complex, mired in the illusion of life. In this model, truly evolved beings don't sully themselves with anger, jealousy and other "negative" emotions. Even so-called positive feelings are negative. Bliss, joy and pleasure are seen as ego attachments.

The emotional equivalent of steamed veggies seems to be neutrality.

Scientists are still studying emotion. For years now, research indicated various hormones and brain biochemistry could explain feelings. If you're depressed, your brain chemistry is "off." If you feel elated, your endorphins are singing. This research formulated the basis for mood-altering medications, which are now prescribed in ever-escalating numbers. A recent (2015) Gallup poll showed almost 20 percent of Americans take a mood-altering drug daily.

New research by neuroscientist Luiz Pessoa suggests the interaction of emotion and cognition in the brain. This validates the ancient teachings that emotion and thought are part of the same thing, although it might take the researchers longer to figure out they are centralized in the heart. Researchers have also discovered a powerful vagus nerve connection between gut bacteria and the brain. Indications are that hormones are released from the gut and that emotion and the quality and type of your gut bacteria are primary factors in emotional health. Here's a link to one of many such studies: http://www.ncbi.nlm.nih.gov/pubmed/21988661. This is called the "gut microbiome," which can reportedly weigh up to 2 kg (about 4 pounds).

The research about emotion is as confusing and contradictory as emotion itself.

From the metaphysical view, feelings are simply energy that arise and move through us, or are stored for later retrieval and processing. Feelings can also be a felt energy from another person, transferred and translated through the chakra system.

Our ever present and changeable feelings are a normal part of human existence. It may be that we are living an illusion and we are all actually deep and quiet essence, but we cannot deny that most of us feel emotions, which go up and down throughout the day. Even our dreams are saturated with feelings.

Thoughts and feelings are often tightly wound around each other. As you listen to the steady drone of your thinking you will inevitably feel associated emotion. This includes feelings felt and "held" by parts of you that have particular beliefs and thought patterns.

In this section we will explore how to feel, heal and release stagnant feelings so you can live an emotionally free life. By emotionally free, I mean that feelings come and go lightly. You neither attach to them, as we all like to do to the ones we enjoy, nor do you ignore them and stuff them down, pretending you are simply "too spiritual" to be angry or sad. The rejection of certain feelings judged as non-spiritual can be called "spiritual bypass."

What is Spiritual Bypass?

"*Spiritual bypass*" is a term coined by John Welwood in the 1970s that describes our human tendency to use spirituality and the pursuit of bliss states to mask or avoid the painful emotions we'd rather ignore. Meanwhile, the emotional truth, pain and negativity live within us, lightly covered with the spiritual veneer.

Proponents of New Age spiritual principles in particular are prone to bypassing through rigid enforcement of positive thought, love and light as the order of the day. Anyone who is depressed, irritable or has a realistic thought might be chided for not being loving or positive enough. Spirituality becomes a straightjacket of pretended feelings, as dangerous and non-empathic to our true selves as punitive, sin-centered old-time religions. In either case we cannot be real.

My beloved teacher John Firman called this same phenomenon *"Transcendental Identity Disorder."* We become identified with transcendent states and with a high spiritual sense of ourselves. We ignore or minimize our personality and humanness.

Many spiritual traditions contain a subtle (and sometimes not-so-subtle) teaching that our goal should be a state in which we disconnect from our humanness, and especially our feelings. We are led to imagine that in our highest state we will be perfect, loving and kind all of the time. Some New Age mystics and Christian groups preach that if you "get it right" you will ascend right off of the earth, leaving your clothes in a pile on the ground while you rise to some fabulous bliss place.

Why is it so hard to live fully within our humanness, accepting all of our parts and all of our emotions? This does not mean we should express our rage and anger in harmful ways, or hold onto grudges and resentments. It simply means we acknowledge that as embodied humans we are capable of all feelings and perspectives, and even terrible actions we'd rather believe we could never do.

As we are able to witness and own the darker potentials in ourselves, the darkness has less power over us. We are able to discern the message—held like a seed—within each feeling. The emotion is a gift. As we explore the connection of current pain to past pain and the limiting threads begin to dissolve, we gain wisdom and compassion. As we accept our human self we find we are no longer so attached, no longer a slave to the ego's endless striving for perfection.

As we face the darkness within ourselves without fear, we free ourselves to explore higher states of joy, creativity, bliss and love. When we cultivate nonattachment to any particularly kind of emotional state, we open up our day-to-day emotional potential to a wider range of comfort. We find a wide, authentic middle range of emotional expression with a natural capacity to experience highs and lows without attachment. We dive deep and fly high.

We don't need to disconnect and leave our body, or pretend to just be a spiritual being, too special for human existence. We'll have plenty of time to experience that state when we've dissolved from the physical plane. We wouldn't have incarnated if that's all we wanted to do. We are meant to embody Spirit fully—on this physical plane—understanding our true power and capacity for bliss and oneness as well as grief and rage and everything in between. This fullness allows us to live a rich, multi-textured authentic life.

The Energy of Emotion

One of the layers of the aura is an emotional body. It is aligned with our feelings. When it is clear, it has a vibrant look and feel which is visible to a skilled clairvoyant. But even if you can't see it yourself, you know when you're around someone with a murky emotional body. They feel "dark." Their energy feels sticky. Perhaps they show their feelings obviously. They are angry, sad, touchy, mean-spirited.

Unresolved, old emotions act as a magnetic blanket around us, attracting negative experiences and challenging people. There is a healing purpose in this. Our current challenging experiences will bring these old feelings up to the surface repeatedly until we face them. As we "see" our feelings clearly and also see the parts of ourselves that hold these feelings, they begin to dissolve and soften. Our emotional field becomes clearer and less stuck.

Fears Manifest What We Are Afraid Of

This is not to say that these feelings are bad, or that it's not okay to feel them. In fact, the exact opposite is true. It's important to feel all of our feelings, in the moment, when we are in situations triggering the feeling.

Think of babies. They cry when they're wet or cold. They scream when they're frustrated or angry. If you can figure out what's wrong with them and correct it, they immediately gurgle and laugh. They are absolutely *in the moment.* Which is how we're all supposed to be. It's challenging to be in the moment when we have stored a casserole of feelings that we weren't at liberty to express when we were young. Or perhaps even now, we've become habituated to repressing certain feelings we consider unacceptable. Perhaps our anger or moodiness will trigger people around us who are even angrier than we are. Perhaps we want to be "spiritual" and always be happy and positive. Maybe we don't even know how to feel our feelings.

I know I was that way myself for many years. I had completely repressed all of my negative feelings as a child, because it wasn't okay in my family to "talk back," to be angry, sad or even questioning. I learned to focus my attention on school and achievements and to act like I was okay. These unexpressed feelings came out later as a need to self-medicate through various addictions. And when I finally went into therapy at age twenty-eight, I was a complete moron about my emotional states. I could feel good or bad, okay or upset. I didn't know the nuanced possibilities of the upset feeling. Was I angry, resentful, afraid, sad? I had absolutely no idea. Therapy 101 was an eye-opener, and I sometimes wonder how my first therapist could stand sitting with me during those first two baby-step years.

A significant part of creating the life you want entails getting in touch with all of your repressed feelings and moving them out of your emotional body.

This does not have to be a long, drawn-out therapy process, although if you have the time and money, therapy can be a true blessing and an amazing gift to yourself. It often takes some time to come to this realization, after the first weeks or months of agonizing visits when parts of yourself absolutely do not want to go, want to quit, hate it.

But, like a good Saturn transit, once you're through it and you've seen, felt and restructured your emotional field, which is simply energy, you are likely to be extremely grateful for what you've endured, what a better life you have and what a better person you are. The tears and gut-wrenching emotional excavations are worth it.

There are many new and developing techniques for working with the emotions energetically and more quickly than traditional talk therapy. EMDR (rapid eye movement therapy performed by some therapists), Buddhist inquiry meditations, psychosynthesis, energetic healing, EFT (Emotional Freedom Technique), Reiki, hypnotherapy, somatic (body-centered) therapies and many more are worth exploring until you find the emotional healing technique that works for you.

Because we're in a period of accelerated growth, the process of healing can be faster than it once was. Just admitting you have unresolved feelings, breathing into them, talking about them, and choosing to stop repressing them, can take you a long way toward having a clearer energy body.

To recap: feeling old feelings and releasing them will free up your emotional energy body so that you can feel current feelings in the moment and act from them with authenticity. When your emotional body is clear and present, you will attract situations and people who are also clearer. From this clarity, you will align more easily with your higher path, no longer drawn into old emotionally-based karmic situations.

Integrating our Parts

A powerful way to address emotional healing is to understand subpersonalities. Personality is made up of many inner parts. These parts range from our inner children at various ages to archetypal figures such as the Achiever, the Lover, the Parent, the Child, the Boss, the Inner Critic or Judge and more. Often many more of these subpersonalities inhabit our psyche, vying for attention and power within us. We've explored some parts already through previous Reflection processes.

These parts were obvious to me as real energies as a psychic channel, even though I knew nothing of the psychological theory. When a person asked a question, the answer would come through as an explanation of the various forces of intention created by the inner parts. This information was both channeled through me from Spirit and was also visible to me clairvoyantly. I would see animated figures moving toward or away from actions. Spirit would say things like, "There is a part of you that wishes to change jobs because it is both bored and likes a new challenge (the Adventurer), yet there is a part of you that is afraid that the new job will not be secure and worries about making a change (the Inner Conservative)."

Rather than just give a yes or no answer, the inner parts and dilemmas would be described along with helpful answers to both parts. There would also be suggestions about how to calm the parts so that the appropriate action could be taken with ease.

I was happily surprised when I found out there was a psychological theory called psychosynthesis that echoed my experiences during years of doing psychic readings. Even more, these parts matched astrological planets in signs and their relationship to each other.

This beautiful theory was created by Roberto Assagioli, an Italian psychiatrist, humanist and visionary. His work has been integrated into humanistic and transpersonal psychology, yet still remains a philosophy in its own right. A living and evolving system, psychosynthesis is practiced by therapists, psychologists and others who continue to follow in Assagioli's path, living the principles, using them in their therapeutic work, teaching and writing. Those who knew him say Assagioli didn't want a formalized school or institution, but rather encouraged his students to go out into the world and simply do psychosynthesis and teach it as they felt called to. Thus, psychosynthesis is somewhat different throughout the world and within various schools and organizations.

He also didn't want his offering to be just for the professionals—it can be taught to anyone. We can learn to be better people, partners, parents, healers or teachers by understanding how subpersonalities have formed and how being seen unconditionally heals and integrates. So much more than inner parts work, the philosophy is infused with the healing power of empathic love. Combined with the rich inner intuitive processes that help us understand more about all of our parts, we are able to heal energetically, emotionally and spiritually in an organic way.

As we learn how to connect with these inner parts as well as Spirit, we become intuitive to all of our "selves." Rather than see our human personality as a problem to avoid or perfect, we begin to truly see who we are and appreciate the parts of ourselves who are young inner children, rebellious teenagers, avid achievers or giving lovers. This includes accepting the various feelings each part has.

We are often told we need to learn to love ourselves before we can receive love or find a partner. Obviously this, like many cultural truisms, turns out not to be totally accurate when we look around at the world. Many people who don't yet love themselves fully are loving to others or have a loving partner, or accept love in some way.

When we connect with ourselves, see our inner parts and understand ourselves without so much judgment—perhaps even with a bit of compassion—we relax into okay-ness. We begin to appreciate who we are. We soften the inner critic or "the Judge" who so often rants in our mind throughout the day.

The process of loving ourselves begins with seeing ourselves as we once wished we could be seen by those around us. Who is this fabulous being living this interesting life? What drives and motivates you? What brings you the most joy and pleasure in life? What is it that calls you? And when you hear the call, are you able to follow?

Grace was pressuring her boyfriend to live with her. They had been dating seriously for over a year and she felt it was time. He said he loved her but didn't feel ready. He was focused on his career, both had been divorced and he felt they should wait at least another year.

As we discussed her conflicted feelings, I asked her to take a breath and feel into the part that was wanting to live together immediately. She described this part as "a part of me that wants to have a bit of a fight, a verbal battle."

Grace said, "This part wants to say things about why I think we should live together now, and be heard. I'm not feeling heard. I'm seeing a part of him that comes out sometimes that is stubbornly clinging to his schedule, his plan, his agenda. See, even as I say 'stubbornly clinging' I am judgmental. I could say how much I love him for his strength, the way he is devoted to his healing plan, his boundary setting that is firm yet loving."

"But this part of mine is very immature, maybe teenage," Grace continued. "She wants to fight about it, even though in a deep place inside I can feel that this is a good decision for him to live alone for a while. I can even see that it's good for me to be alone a while longer too, and I feel ultimately we'll live together. The relationship is just so very good, how could we not choose that?"

"So, I know it's all good, but I still want a verbal battle," said Grace. "What is the point of that? I already plan to concede. It just adds to his feeling of being pressured by me and not supported 100 percent."

I ask what this part looks like. "She's wearing black leather with metal hardware, very hipster, punk, dyke," she said. "She's about twenty-two and immature but thinks she's cool. She wants a lot of attention, but she's impatient. She will demand a relationship and moves quickly, as twenty-year-olds do, without knowing someone. She acts independent but she's fairly needy sometimes."

I ask, "What does she need?"

Grace responds: "I see her dragging a huge black mass, carried over her shoulder, like a monster on a stick. She doesn't know she has value in life, and in relationship, so she's always trying to make it work, to drag someone in."

When I ask what needs to happen next, Grace tells her she can let go of the burden. She can trust that Mark or someone will come to her. The relief is huge in her chest. She tears up. As we talk she realizes the black burden comes from abuse, energies all confused, no sense of her specialness. As she softens, this inner teenager's clothes don't have so many spikes and her makeup is more subdued. Her inner four-year-old (discovered in a previous session) takes her hand. She feels peaceful.

It helps to have someone guide you through such a process, but you can learn to do it yourself in meditation, developing a healing relationship with your inner parts.

The Process of Exploring Subpersonalities

In the Reflection section, I will give you a short and easy meditation to help you connect to a subpersonality. This section will give you a deeper overview of how it works.

Begin by getting into a comfortable position, free of distractions for at least fifteen minutes. You might like to do subpersonality work in the bathtub because of the calming influence of hot water and perhaps add some relaxing essential oil. You might also like to close your eyes to focus inward more easily.

Think of a situation in your life that is causing you uncomfortable feelings or a challenge in making a choice. You can focus on strong feelings even if you don't yet know clearly what they're about. The feelings could be anger, fear, abandonment fear, anxiety, depression, resentment and so on. Pick the feeling you'd like to work on, and then breathe slowly with an intention to connect to that feeling in your body.

You will ask the part of you that is holding these feelings to "separate" from you so that you can see it and learn more about it. Or, more simply, imagine the part of you that is feeling this way as a person, perhaps like a cartoon character or overly-exaggerated image. Sometimes a part shows up as an energy: like a black cloud or a small tight stick on the ground.

As you "see" this image in your mind, notice in more detail what this person/part is like. Does it have other feelings? What does it remind you of? What sorts of things does it like to do (or not do) in your life? Get a sense of what this part wants. Ask or feel into what it actually needs.

An inner part might tell you it wants to be in a relationship. It might be emphatic that it wants to be in relationship with a particular person. But the bottom-line need is simply love. When we want a new job, the driving need might be acknowledgment or power, or financial security.

The truth about an inner part's need will come to you intuitively as you explore the question: "What is your essential need?"

Once you have determined the inner need, consider how that need might be fulfilled energetically. You are working co-creatively in energetic/psychic space with this part now, as if this is a beloved friend. You might have an idea yourself of what is needed and be able to offer it. For instance, if the part is an inner child who needs love and security, you might reach out your adult hand and offer to hold this child. Or maybe you don't feel ready for that; you can suggest that a "wise and loving being" come into the picture to hold the child. This being might show up like an angel or Spirit or a favorite grandmother or aunt. Other times it's just an energy that's needed: a feeling of love or security or a color.

As you bring healing energy to this part, there may be a change in the way the part looks. The child softens and relaxes. An angry part shrinks and begins to smile. A stressed part dances to let off steam and lets you know you too need to dance in your "real" world.

You'll know intuitively when you're complete with the process. You can ask the part if there is anything it wants you to do in your daily life so it knows you care about it. Some parts wish we'd play or create, or stay away from certain people. Listen to the message and find a way to accommodate the need if that is possible for you. Sometimes there's another part within you that is absolutely against the part you're working with. You can work with that part next, either in the same meditation or at a different time.

These inner processes seem very clear when we're in them, but because we are working in energetic/psychic space, we will normally forget the details fairly rapidly. It is a good idea to write everything down in a journal as soon as possible after the process, or even during, if you're able to meditate, see and write at the same time.

#13 - REFLECTION

1. Meditation #13.1: Emotion

Place yourself in a comfortable position with a straight spine. Direct your breath in a focused way from head to toe as if you are scanning your body with the intention to discover emotion. When you find a feeling that feels strong or interesting, breathe into it. Do not try to change it or resist it. Simply breathe into it. In your mind you can name the feeling: anger, anxiety, mild happiness, frustration, etc. As you breathe into the feeling, sometimes a picture arises in your mind of the nature of the energy of the feeling. Allow the picture to formulate, noticing various details, and allow it to change if it wants to. Stay with the feeling for as long or as short a time as you wish. You can also imagine what the energy looks like: color, shape, edges, density.

Often, the feeling will change. If it does and you notice the change, you can name the new feeling. An example would be that anger is sometimes the presenting emotion, and underneath you will find sadness. Perhaps then sadness shifts to vulnerability. Usually after some time of breathing into the feeling, there is a sense of calm. You have come to the end of this exploration. Allow your intuitive-felt sense to guide you.

2. Meditation #13.2: Release Emotion in Water

Place your body in a comfortable position. Imagine you are in water, like a warm tropical pool, or even a bathtub. You can even do this meditation in the bathtub or a hot tub. Imagine the water is magical and it can dissolve and melt stuck and stored feelings in your body. Breathe into your body, moving the breath from place to place, imagining and watching as the breath and the water melt old stored emotion. You might imagine you can see the water turning a dark color, like an oil spill, as the emotion melts and releases. Watch the dark energy swirl away, down the drain or out through a stream away from the pool.

When you feel empty, take deep breaths from over your head, drawing on the vibration of your essence as it enters through a gateway approximately twelve to eighteen inches over the top of your head. Finally, fill yourself up with pure, clear Light.

3. Meditation #13.3: Subpersonality Process

Identify an emotion you wish to know more about or heal. Begin the meditation in a comfortable position, spine straight. Breathe slowly yet naturally. Close your eyes. Imagine you are outside in nature in a beautiful setting. Take some time to feel this place in every way, smelling the scent in the air, hearing sounds in the background, and feeling the breeze on your skin, as well as seeing the colors and shapes of nature all around you. Find a place to rest.

Ask the part of you that holds the emotion to separate from you, like a cartoon figure, energy formation or an image of a person (this could look like you or not). The part of you that is an observer simply "sees" this part that holds the emotion and notices:

1.   How does this part look physically, or if the image isn't clear, how would it look if you could see it?
2.   What kind of mood or emotional attitude might it have in addition to the core emotion you asked about? (It's possible the part that comes out actually has a different emotion).

3. What does it need?
4. What is its essential need?
5. Can you meet this need or would you like to call in a Wise and Loving Being, or even an energy? For example, if the part needs love, you can reach out and offer a hug, call in a Loving Being, or just imagine a loving breeze of light surrounding the part.
6. Check to see if there's anything else the part wants to do or say.
7. Imagine this part of you—and the whole picture—gently returning to your interior.

4. Reflection for Journaling

Observe yourself throughout the day. What emotional quality or mood is your set point, or comfortable range of emotion? Do you find yourself experiencing joy, laughter, bliss and peace? Do you find yourself experiencing sadness, grief, despair, rage? Feel your emotion without trying to hang onto it or repress it. Journal about your experience.

CHAPTER FOURTEEN

The Physical Pillar

*"To embody is to steep yourself in the endless
exploration of the physical."*
—Janet Stone

The physical pillar of healing includes care and tending of the body and the cultivation of sacred space around us. Physical space includes rooms, homes and offices, plus connection to the vibrant power of nature. The physical also includes the actions we take. Do you feel grounded and whole in your body? Can you manifest the higher levels of will to act in alignment with your truth? Let's look at these areas one by one.

Body

The skeleton forms the center of the physical body. Surrounded by flesh, filled with precious organs, the soul of you has manifested energy into a unique temple to be the vehicle for this journey. It seems real, semi-solid and permanent throughout life, but actually it's a mirage of swirling molecules and tiny particles.

This apparent physicality pretends to be something solid, like a house, a truck or a mountain. But if you've ever been in an earthquake and seen the waves of concrete ripple beneath you, you know nothing is actually solid at all. In an earthquake you watch the floor flow in waves like a rolling ocean surf. When the quake stops and that massive, corrective energy shift beneath the earth is complete, you hope the floors and walls simply go back to their regular flat, straight physical shape. If the force is too great, there will be cracks.

If you've seen that, physicists don't have to prove to you that there's something magical about form. It seems soft, hard, plush, brittle, heavy or gossamer light, but all of physical creation is made from energy. Quantum physics has now proven what Indian masters and even Socrates said thousands of years ago. It is all energy. Scientists have peered inside of atoms, the building block of form: they discovered waves of energy. This energy moves randomly, but also responds to the thought of the scientist, even if he or she is not in the room.

This is so cool.

As we absorb the new science that is also ancient truth, our understanding of physicality dissolves. Physical structures are not as fixed as we imagined them to be. Even the hardest concrete can be changed with thought.

Martial arts exhibitions also demonstrate the magic of energy, intention and thought. My hand screams in terror to even imagine breaking bricks. Obviously it can't be the force of muscles or the tiny bones impacting hard surfaces. Most of us would break our wrists and hand bones punching even one brick. We'd bleed. Somehow martial artists channel a force of energy greater than solid matter to split bricks or boards in half. How do they do it?

The practice slowly and methodically cultivates energy. The mind is trained to believe it is possible. Energy responds to thought. Single-minded thought and focused energy are stronger than whatever apparent strength is holding together a mass of energy called wood or brick.

How can we work with the world of form in a more elegant way? Might we be able to change our health and physical body shape through thought and focused intention? Geneen Roth's powerful work on body image says yes. Be loving, kind and curious with yourself to heal your relationship with food and your body. It's not about what you eat; it's the thoughts, emotions and inner relationship you cultivate.

Elite athletes also work with these concepts when they are injured. If they visualize their workout practice while they are recuperating, the body heals faster and they don't lose their conditioning.

The evidence is growing that we can heal or re-create our bodies through positive thought. As we'll discuss in more detail later, creation energy responds to subconscious thoughts, not just the conscious "I am thin" or "my health is vibrant." We create our bodies through thoughts we may not be aware of. Reflection time spent uncovering this process often excavates surprising underlying creation blueprints.

Not that eating well won't help. It will, although the definition of "well" is complex and fraught with conflicting beliefs. Vegetarian, paleo, vegan, macrobiotic, calorie counting, Mediterranean . . . the list of theories is endless. Then there is the *energy* of food that often transcends the value of exactly what we eat. Never eat the food of an angry chef: do you know who prepared your food and how they were feeling? Are you sensitive enough to notice the energetics of your tomato basil salad? Are you eating the sad energy of semi-slave farm workers? Or the stressed out, underpaid line cooks behind the scenes?

You've probably read a million articles and books about your body and health, so I'm not going to repeat it all. We have serious dietary information overload. We've become overwhelmed and confused by the constantly shifting advice, the faulty research, the newest trends.

Physical sanity requires that you get in touch with your body in an intuitive way and listen to yourself. The inner doctor is there, on call, at all times. Not that you can fix everything yourself, especially when you've ignored warning signals for too long. But the voice inside that says you shouldn't eat that second whatever, or that it's time to get a checkup, or that, well, something is just wrong inside, is your intuitive guide for body health.

Listen to your body and do what your body asks you to do. Health can be that simple.

I've known several friends who were diagnosed with cancer who all had a feeling something was wrong with their body well before anything turned up in medical testing.

Deb had headaches for months. She stopped eating gluten and sugar, got massages, and tried to relax. Her acupuncturist didn't see that anything major was wrong. Deb went for all kinds of medical tests that turned up nothing before the brain tumor finally showed itself.

I neglected to pursue a strong urge to get foot reflexology for about a year before an earthquake injury tore the soft tissue in my foot—forcing me to have extensive foot reflexology in the healing process. I have often wondered if I could have avoided that injury by listening and acting the initial intuition. Instead I "sort of" listened. I asked my regular massage therapists to do extra work on my feet during the year before the injury, but the message from my body was specifically "get foot reflexology"— and I ignored it.

If you want to hear your body's intuition you have to slow down and listen—and then act on what you hear, even when it sounds crazy.

One of the things our bodies tell us is what to eat. We get very specific messages in the form of lightness and energy or dullness after each bite. When we override this intuitive truth again and again, and eat foods that are not great fuel for our unique body, we are creating illness rather than vibrancy and health.

Are you eating the right diet for you? Do you know what your body likes, and how it shifts with the seasons? Are you taking herbs or supplements that work for you, or does life get in the way? Can you find a balance between pleasurable eating and healthy eating, uniquely for you? Is there anyone on the planet who doesn't know daily exercise is essential for a well-functioning body? The American government has been afraid to tell us how much exercise is actually beneficial, because getting people to move from couch potato status to three thirty-minute walks a week was a big enough stretch. It's becoming clear that constant movement throughout each day *plus* more strenuous exercise every day would be optimal. Again, your unique needs will be clear to you when you give yourself a chance to listen to your inner healers.

Yoga, Tai Chi and other meditative arts heal in profound ways with the added benefit of merging spirituality with physicality. Movement, mindfulness and breath together form a radical opponent to diseases of non-movement and incorrect fuel for the body. Any movement you love to do can be a meditative physical exercise. Find what works for you and what fits in your schedule. Use your favorite music to help energize you as you move and begin to live lovingly in your body.

One of the energetic laws of manifestation is that whatever we don't like or are afraid of becomes more deeply stuck. This is particularly evident with the tendency to dislike and criticize parts of our bodies. It's challenging to change your body in any way when you hate it. It's hard to create vibrant health when you resent your celery-and-flaxseed smoothie. This is why the process needs to be intuitive and loving, and usually slower than faster. A slow, steady approach toward loving and listening to the body while making small incremental shifts of life choices usually works better than drill-sergeant diets and exercise regimens that don't actually fit in your life.

If you can't love your body, at least try to make friends with it. Find a body part you *can* accept . . . your little finger? Your shapely calves? Then focus your love and appreciation on them. If you can, develop a relationship with your whole body to appreciate it, as it is, without necessarily having to change it. Change occurs through love and acceptance.

Kimber Simpkins' fantastic memoir *Full* explores body image with a beautiful approach to consciously connecting with our bodies and a healthier more vibrant relationship to food. It's essential reading for women—many of us have such crazy body issues. We've been squished, harmed and criticized endlessly, directly and indirectly. How can we live from a soul-centered life, accomplish our mission, and enjoy each moment, when we're secretly obsessing about our thighs, cellulite, wrinkles and endless "problems" manufactured by the people who want to sell us stuff?

The inner work around body image takes time, but there is a movement afoot now that finally begins to support loving acceptance of body differences.

Restore Yourself

One of the most amazing things you can do for your health is simple restorative yoga. A supported savasana "nap" is a restful meditation that will allow your nervous system to reset and heal in a way that is different from sleep. In sleep, your body is busy recalibrating and repairing cells. The brain is in overdrive processing your emotional life. A healing yogic nap can replace your habitual 4:00 p.m. craving for more caffeine or a snack. A simple set up includes a pillow under your knees, a soft, low support under the neck, and an eye pillow to block out light. Set the timer for twenty minutes. That's it. You'll find more details in the Reflection section.

If you are a sensitive person with a strong aptitude for psychic development, there's a good chance that your nervous system can become frazzled on occasion. "Frazzled" isn't actually a solid medical term, and hopefully you can feel the condition of your nervous system before it becomes a medical issue, called a "nervous breakdown." But "frazzled" describes well the feeling of being tense, irritable and ungrounded that occurs when psychic sensitivity is on overload.

The symptoms of a tired nervous system include:

- *Headaches, especially in the forehead*

- *A sizzling feeling in the head*

- *Lack of focus or concentration*

- *Difficulty sleeping*

- *Irritability (especially when it is uncharacteristic)*

This is how it usually happens. You attend a psychic development class or read a book and begin to meditate more often than ever before. You have discovered your Spirit guides and love receiving messages from them, whether for yourself or for friends. Perhaps you've learned about meditating with high-frequency colors of light: white, gold or silver. When you imagine bringing these exalted colors into your aura you feel wonderful feelings of bliss and calmness.

All is going well for weeks or even months, and then suddenly you find yourself irritable and edgy, unable to sleep at night even when you feel tired. Your nervous system feels kind of burned out, edgy and stressed.

Nervous system burnout can and does happen to seasoned intuitives. It occurs when you're sensitive and overly busy with life, especially when living in urban environments. Perhaps you have had a few nights with too little sleep or a challenging travel schedule. Or you have a virus coming on. If you continue to do high-frequency meditations or other activities that stress the nervous system, you'll feel it. My red flag is that suddenly I douse my conversation with four-letter words, which is not typical for me. Or perhaps I'm more impatient in traffic. That's how I know I've lost my center. My energy has gone from calm and light to edgy and dark. It happens quite quickly.

Here's another example:

Cynthia was a young psychic student whom I recognized as gifted from the very first class. She was delighted to be offered a spot at a local crystal shop doing readings on Saturday afternoons. The readings were twenty minutes long and allowed ten-minute breaks between sessions. But Cynthia had a hard time keeping to the twenty minutes. It was all so exciting. Most days each reading went over into her break so that her sessions were back-to-back. At first she just felt tired. But after some time she found she couldn't sleep at night. She became anxious and irritable. Before, she had loved physical activity of all kinds and had an active job. Now she found herself staying in the house with the blinds drawn, truly unable to function. When she finally reached out to me to ask what had happened, her journey back to balance was long and challenging. She had to give up doing readings and focus on healing her body and nervous system for many months.

The energy in Cynthia's aura or chakras at that time had a tense and tight feel to it and her grounding into the Earth was poor. A burned-out nervous system is hot and dry, so the healing recipe begins with water:

1. **Bath.** Add one cup of baking soda to the bath, along with a few drops of essential lavender oil. A tablespoon or so of coconut oil will sit on top of the water and add a moisturizing and healing touch. Soak in this bath, especially lying down so that your head is covered by water,

leaving your face open to breathe. The water around the head is especially calming.

2. **Shower.** A second option is a shower—although if your nervous system is acutely stressed, the feeling of water beating on your body may feel too intense.

3. **Stop Meditations.** Stop any type of stimulating or psychic-style meditation for now. It's okay to do basic breathing meditation, yoga or Tai Chi.

4. **Physical Exercise.** Exercise is particularly helpful to balance a stressed nervous system, get back in the body and become more grounded. Choose any exercise you feel personally drawn to, although yoga, Tai Chi and Qigong are notable for their balancing of energy along with physical exercise. Try walking, running, Zumba, dancing, swimming, weights and cardio work at the gym . . . anything you like. Make sure to focus on breathing slowly and deeply, feeling your breath touch into the lower parts of your body to become grounded again.

5. **Nature.** Get outside. Take off your shoes and walk on bare earth, especially dirt or grass that's slightly damp, because moisture transmits energy. Called "Earthing," proponents say your whole energy system is rejuvenated and reset in eighty minutes through direct contact with the Earth.

6. **Colored lights.** Soft, cool colors such as pinks, blues and greens are soothing and healing to the nervous system. Place a "party" bulb in a lamp and bathe in the joy of color vibration. Avoid strong, hot colors such as red or orange.

7. **Stones and Crystals**. Learn about grounding stones like hematite, black onyx and others. Wear them in jewelry or carry a small stone in your pocket to repel psychic energies and relax the nervous system. Note that wearing too many high-frequency stones can cause additional problems. Keep it simple and aim for balance.

Space

Your home, office, cars and other physical spaces are also manifested by your intentions. How do you take care of your space? Have you created an environment that nurtures your soul? Your physical space is like the grand temple that surrounds your personal body temple.

Does your physical space support your life's mission and dreams? Consider that your exterior space is a reflection of your inner harmony and integrity. Simplicity, beauty and ease of use might be primary qualities you'd want to consider. But maybe not. Each of us has an ideal vision of space. You might be sharing space with family, friends, partners, and four-legged friends. Despite the benefits of companionship, you might have a longing for your own space exactly as you like it. That can be on your wish list, available to manifest as space permits. There can be an interesting split between what we would love ideally and our current reality. Your home doesn't have to be fancy, but it should reflect your taste and comfort levels. In our Western world, usually we have too much stuff—the opposite is rare.

There are many theories of how to simplify, pare down and organize yourself. I particularly love Marie Kondo's book *The Life-Changing Magic of Tidying Up* to help release possessions and organize yourself to core essentials. Her connection to the feelings of clothes and other objects tickles my psychic sensitivities.

Create your secure sanctuary. Your meditation and inner-development processes need a safe, secure sanctuary. This might be a room set aside for this purpose, or an altar in a corner of a room. Another kind of sanctuary could be a padded lounge chair on your patio, surrounded by fragrant lavender and crimson geraniums. A cup of tea and a soft furry friend on your lap completes the vibe. You decide. You can have little pockets of sanctuary in every room.

Place pictures of spiritual beings, statues, incense, and crystals in your sanctuary. Burn sage in this room regularly. Called "smudging," you burn the end of a wrapped bundle of sage for a moment until the end releases some smoke. Walk through your space waving the smoke to the corners, windows and doors. Intention is as important as the sage itself. "May all who enter be filled with love," or another positive expression of healing affirmation is great to use at the doorways. Once you have burned away the heavier energy, allowed the breeze to wash through by opening doors and windows, set positive intent, and light sweetgrass or a sweet incense. Burn candles regularly to invite in light energies and discourage the dark. *Be very careful* to completely put the sage out and monitor all burning flames. More than once I've thought my smudge stick was out and found myself sitting in a room filled with smoke twenty minutes later. Once I lived in an apartment where once the smoke alarms were triggered, only the fire department could turn them off. The firefighters were courteous, but truly not amused.

Purify your Space. If you are spending time in someone else's physical space, or if you notice an extra level of dark energy in your room or home, try these healing processes.

1. Visualize a white sheet of energy under the building or room you're in. Imagine drawing the sheet up through the space by the four corners. Imagine it as a sieve that collects the heavy energy in the space. When the sheet rises above the building, all the heaviness is inside of the sheet and you can tie up the corners and toss it up into the stars. Ask for Spirit help to do this.

2. Visualize gold light in the walls, floors and ceiling of your space. Imagine the gold in the walls going deep into the Earth to create a firm foundation.

3. Visualize a crystal pyramid over the entire building and land, maybe even over your entire community. Feel its protective energy beaming down on your space.

4. The old-fashioned approach is to simply clean your house with natural cleaning products. Cleaning physically removes old, stuck, dark energy from physical space.

5. Clapping. Walk through your rooms clapping your hands, especially in corners, to break up stuck energy. You'll be surprised by how well clapping works.

Earth

The ground beneath us, our precious Earth, can be seen as part of our physical pillar of healing. Our body is supported by the Earth's body. We are healed by the vast energetic currents running through the land—or we are sickened by a planet that is struggling. It can be heartbreaking to see the escalating loss and devastation of our Earth-body, yet encouraging to see efforts made toward renewal and healing. We have the opportunity at this crucial point in history to become part of a collaborative healing process—or we can turn away in delusion and despair. Earth has an amazing capacity to transform herself, although her somewhat psychopathic personal healing process can be devastating to all of the life-forms who would prefer to continue living on her surface. Gaia will survive. But the fate of humankind and the vast diversity of plants, animals and birds is questionable. Apparently the insects have it covered.

If all matter is created by thought, then somewhere, somehow, we, or someone, created Earth. It follows that if we can create this luxurious beauty and billions of symbiotic species, we can surely dream-create a sustainable Earth space for future generations. We are not limited by what we've done so far.

Picture yourself in a vibrant place in nature. What is your ideal? Tropical and fragrant? Frosty snow and the pure clean air of the mountains? Your body was made to connect with nature. Without regular time outside there's a part of your energy form that starts to contract. A recent Stanford University study showed that when research participants walked for ninety minutes, half of them in nature and the other half in an urban environment, the ones who walked through a park had lower levels of blood flow to the part of the brain that's involved in rumination—that pesky habit of negative thinking.

Action

Finally, take daily actions to maintain your connection with soul path. Conscious thought, direct action in alignment with plans, letting go of habitual actions—the simple choices we make every day affect personal manifestation of form.

Do we have to take action? Or will positive thinking and being in the flow of our path allow everything we need to occur spontaneously?

I believe both matter. At the core of being in the physical world, we know that our thoughts, words and actions manifest reality. What we think is always being broadcast, even if we don't know we're thinking it. Our words—both written and spoken— have a stronger energetic vibration. Actions speak louder than words, as they say.

Actions must be consistent with true path for the best results. In this way, action matters a lot. If you say you want to accomplish one of your soul path goals, but the actions you're taking are not on that path, at all, you are sending out mixed messages to the causal plane, the energetic plane of existence that is constantly in creation mode.

When you take an action, *be* the action with your whole self. When you learn to uni-task, a concept completely out of the norm in our crazy paced world, you relax just a little and ultimately get more done. As you wash the dishes, can you feel the warmth of the water on your hands, the delight of soap bubbles? Can your thoughts be of gratitude for having dishes, and food, and a kitchen—rather than mindless running of thought, especially worry and circular thinking? Simple attention to each moment opens up a world of pleasure in living. Life thrives with richness when we attend to the details with clear, mindful presence. Action is a key component of a healthy physical existence.

REFLECTION #14

FOR THE BODY

1. Ayurvedic Warm Oil Massage . . . with loving intention

Warm up sesame or coconut oil. If it's in an airtight container, you can place it in a bowl of hot water and it will warm within a few minutes. You can also purchase an oil warmer. Take the time to massage your whole body with warm oil, with as much appreciation and care as you can cultivate. If you can intentionally love and adore your body, that's great. Just start where you are, with appreciation for having a body and the intention to be healing and caring.

B. SAVASANA NAP

Lie down with a bolster, large pillow or two regular pillows under your knees. Use a small pillow or folded towel to support your neck. The idea is to support a gentle curve of the neck so that the chin is neither wide open nor crunched to the chest. Place an eye pillow or folded small towel over your eyes. Set your alarm timer for twenty to thirty minutes. Place your hands on your thighs or flat beside you, palms up. Breathe slowly and consciously, feeling the gentle rise and fall of the belly. If you notice thoughts, bring your attention back to feeling the breath; watching the inhale and exhale.

It's okay if you fall asleep. It will be brief, refreshing and well-needed. If you surrender to a deep, heavy resting state, that too is great. A savasana nap can produce a deep consciousness of some awareness while resting—the place between asleep and awake. If your mind won't turn off and you can't relax, this is a sign that you'll need more time to lower your stress level. Be patient with yourself. Although savasana is a yogic practice, naps are enjoyed in many cultures, as siestas or long family lunch hours at home. Enjoying a conscious savasana every day allows the body to restore and heal, and teaches us to relax deeply to balance with the activity of daily life.

FOR SPACE
3. Meditation #14.1: Purify a Space
In this meditation guidance, I will use "room" as the type of space you are purifying, but this could also be a whole house, a hotel room, a commercial space or office.

1. Begin with your basic breathing meditation to center yourself, calling on your Spirit Guides and helpers to help you if you wish.
2. Imagine a beautiful white or golden blanket under the room.
3. Draw the blanket up through the room, like a sieve. Imagine you are trapping negative energies within this blanket. Draw the corners together when it is through the room, asking healing Spirits to take it to the cosmos for purification.
4. Then visualize golden Light in the floor, walls and ceiling.
5. Imagine a beautiful color of healing Light "raining" into the room.
6. Imagine a crystal pyramid suspended in space over the room or building.
7. Feel the power of who you are as a soul in this space and set intention that only the Light may enter.

WITH THE EARTH

4. Soul Path Offering: Walk with Your Inner Child:
Go to a park or walking trail. Sit for a couple of minutes to
breathe mindfully, and connect with your inner child (any
age under 10). Then walk slowly with deep connection to
your child. See the natural world through the eyes of your
inner child.

TAKE ACTION

5. Journal Reflection: Mission and Action

Look at your Mission statement and sub-goals. Think
about the way you spend your time each day, each week.

Are you taking actions that are in alignment with your
goals?

Where are you wasting time, doing things you'd actually rather not do or know are not your best choices? What
changes would you like to make?

Small tweaks and adjustments create great results.

Journal about your thoughts, without judgment. Imagine you are a loving life/business consultant to yourself.
What small steps could you take?

Part Four

MANIFESTATION & CO-CREATION

CHAPTER FIFTEEN

Divine Creation

"Can I manifest what I want, when I want?
Or should I change my desires so that I'm sat-
isfied with what I already have?"

We all want stuff. Creatures of desire and habit, easily influenced by friends, family and media, we dream up things we
want and try to get them. TVs and cars, furniture and food, designer
this and bargain that. Fantasies of lying on a beach with a piña co-
lada dressed with a tiny paper umbrella, or immersed to our chin
in a swirling spa tub, our minds continually tell us what we need
and what we want. We imagine we'll be happy when we get the
next thing or the last thing. And truly, we are thrilled when we peel
the sparkly wrappings off the latest toy, or dress up in the latest
fashion, whether our taste runs to Neiman Marcus, thrift shops or
Lululemon. The thrill fades within minutes, days or weeks. Meanwhile we're already engaged in the search for the next acquisition.

Beyond physical possessions and pleasure, we want love, friends, security, work, meaningful work, a career, promotions, more money, more promotions, more clients, our own TV show...

I want. I need. I desire. I hope for. I wish ...

Endless wheel.

What are we to do? Should we give it all up? Most spiritual traditions suggest the benefits of living simply with minimal or no possessions. Meditation can quell the incessant mind chatter, slowing down the desire/thought mind machine.

If you're not inclined to harness your desires for spiritual reasons, the "voluntary simplicity" movement suggests we can find greater joy and ease by paring down and living with less: change the voracious desire settings, turn down the volume and say no to the (possibly) spoiled child. Plus theoretically, if we use less resources there will be more to share with the rest of the world.

Joe Dominguez and Vicki Robin wrote the inspirational book *Your Money or Your Life,* published in 1992. They teach a method for calculating how much your life is actually costing you. For instance, you may think you're earning $80,000 a year, but once you take away your clothing (work costume) expenses, commuting, restaurant lunches, and the need for an expensive vacation to reward yourself for working so hard . . . in the end you're actually not making as much as you thought.

Many of us live like slaves to subconscious choices made years ago. We set ourselves up in a life that requires an endless amount of work from the time we're in our twenties until we retire. College debt, home mortgage, car payments, children and their needs—paying for life as previously constructed with very little possibility of change. These life choices are often brewed out of imprinted expectations without enough conscious consideration beforehand.

Dominguez and Robin propose the ideal of paying off all debt by living simply to buy yourself the luxury of time. Once you learn to live within a modest, frugal budget, you can live off investment income, or work a minimal amount of time doing something you love. Life choices can buy freedom to live as you wish, or endless debt and hard work to pay for things you've already forgotten. You can create a life that is not an endless treadmill by choosing simplicity.

Happily, some changes are afoot. The youngest generations are trying to change this culture of life as endless work by demanding flexible hours and extra vacations. Forward-thinking companies (who need young, creative employees) are promoting a radical new approach to work life. Bed/couches in offices, free lunches, liberal vacations, basketball courts, and many other perks retain employees and offer more balance. Many of these companies also feed the instant wealth desire by offering stock options and retention bonuses. If your company goes public, you win big. Otherwise you've been working sixteen hours a day, with a flexible schedule that is a questionable incentive. Your office bed has a well-used look to it. You are thirty-five years old but already tired and burned out. You're stuck on the endless wheel unless you happen to win that magic stock-payoff lottery.

Self-employment is an appealing alternative to the corporate work train, yet that can entail even longer hours and precarious financial stress.

It's no surprise then that we find theories of positive thinking as a way to manifest wealth and comfort so appealing. The idea that we can create wealth through positive thought and mind control has captured our attention, shown by the popularity of authors like Catherine Ponder, Esther Hicks, and Mike Dooley. The film *The Secret* blasted these ideas into mainstream awareness in 2006. This documentary deepened the cultural imagination and brought thought-magic out of the closet. Yet the strong emphasis on manifesting money and houses and the hype that it's simple to do left some cold. After all, if it was that easy, wouldn't we all be lying around our mansion's pool with our perfect bodies by now?

Do these techniques not work because we don't want to manifest stuff as much as we think we do? Or is it that we aren't trying hard enough, or not being consistent? I've been pondering and observing these questions for a long time and it comes down to two issues:

1.   *What do you truly want?*

2.   *Who are You? What part of you is choosing?*

What *do* you truly want? Simple, spiritual living or the magical manifestation of a twelve-bedroom mansion? Where do you want to put your precious energy? If you want power, success, money, horses and hot dates, you *can* have it all . . . ***if it's in alignment with your soul's path***. And that's the catch.

If all that worldly fun stuff is not in alignment with your soul's path, all the diligent positive thought you can muster won't be enough to manifest it. If you have deep emotional blockages to accomplishing your aims, they will sabotage your thoughts too.

High-Self Mind is the source of your original path. This is who you truly are—the source that projected your original thought vibration before you were born into the physical. This "you" chose this life. Manifestation originates from this pure soul place within. Your (low) self-mind, the thought process of the ego, has the option to work with or against the flow.

If a desired accomplishment is in alignment with your soul's path, and your negative ego thoughts and beliefs that you don't deserve it are holding you back, then positive thought and manifestation processes *will* work for you. If, on the other hand, your ego wants stuff and your Soul wants to grow and evolve in a different way, working through the seven steps I'm about to outline will help clarify and heal the places where you're split so that you either accomplish the goals or realize what your truer goals are.

It's a win-win.

When you are in alignment with your path, you don't need to *do* anything. Everything you need comes to you lavishly and before you can even think of it.

Learning manifestation techniques are necessary because we have lost our sense of creative power through erroneous imprinting. Like going back to learn intuitive skills, most of us need to understand these powerful creative principles. We need to learn how to skillfully manifest events in the material world. Only then can we forget about them and surf the flow.

When you are stuck in desire and you're not getting what you want, the manifestation principles I'm about to share will help you heal, create and let go.

Manifesting and the Laws of Attraction

When I first worked with the basic concepts for prosperity and manifesting, the teachings were exciting and resonated deeply for me and the students I was working with. But over time, I noticed that people kept working on the same ideas over and over again, not able to create what they wanted. They didn't reach their goals with enough regularity to be certain that positive thinking was paying off. Or they created what they thought they wanted and it turned out not to be so great. They were stuck on an endless New Year's resolution hamster wheel.

The complete secret to how life works in a creative and spiritual way is nuanced and integrated.

The core philosophy that thought creates reality is absolutely true. Negative thoughts, emotions, old patterns and the mass consciousness of the world affect the way thoughts can create. The Mind that is creating is more than personal ego mind. Creation works best when we're in alignment with our true path and live from a place of clarity of mind and emotions, with just the right balance between metaphysical focus and physical actions.

The Seven Steps to Successful Creation

"The mind is like a garden . . . you choose
what to grow: weeds or flowers."
— from *The Dalai Lama's Cat* by Michie Page

Many people use some variation of this quote about the mind being like a garden, but I prefer to think of it as coming from a cat, one of the most zen animals we are pleasured to know. Lying around in the sun, demanding their ideal food, napping endlessly, cats are truly feline savasana masters. They have figured out how to have a fairly decent life for the most part, trading on their ability to grow soft fur and to purr, traits they determined we humans go crazy for.

Is it domesticated cats who gave us the idea life should be easy, or did we always have this fantasy? One of the biggest confusions people have originates from a core belief that life is meant to be secure, easy and flowing all of the time if they're "doing it right." The fact that our souls are playful, courageous vibrations dabbling in all life has to offer, including pain and misery, just doesn't make sense. We begin to feel that the "Universe"—or "God" or "everyone"—is against us, or that we are doing something wrong when we find ourselves feeling block or stuck.

As we explore creation principles, I invite you to hold an overview that everything we experience as humans is part of a continually unfolding process. When we release strong opinions of good and bad, and constant judgment, we open ourselves to more flow.

We must connect to our purpose, and then work through various healing steps to dissolve old patterns. To create consciously we have to strengthen new ways of thinking, speaking and acting. We can release emotional blockages and take positive actions toward our new, soul centered goals. And then . . .

We have no elegant choice but to accept with equanimity the experiences we are faced with every day. To struggle against reality simply doesn't work out very well. It's necessary to accept what is, integrated with a new way of seeing, a new way of thinking. Perhaps a new action. Slowly and with intention we move toward "goals" while honoring the current moment with its joy, pain and endless change.

"Do not dwell in the past, do not dream of the future,
concentrate the mind on the present moment."
—Buddha

To live a creative, spiritually-focused life, it's helpful to have a philosophical understanding of the underlying energy with which we all work. Creation includes manifesting within the stream of the soul's ideal path, yet before that can happen we have to figure out just exactly what that is. So hopefully by now as you've worked through the earlier Reflections you do have a sense of your soul path, and the steps you'd like to accomplish.

It doesn't make much sense to work at manifesting a promotion at a boring job when your heart joyfully sings at the thought of becoming a performing musician or writing a best-selling book. Perhaps you are a healer at your core and you're wondering how to be true to yourself but still pay the bills. Or perhaps you love the excitement and financial benefits of the career you've chosen, but would like to feel balanced with a sense of Spirit infusing your day-to-day life.

Manifestation is not just about using principles to create "items" that the ego wants. Manifesting material things and desired events can be good practice in the learning process but it doesn't usually lead to deeper satisfaction or spiritual growth.

On a soul level, we are powerful, creative beings. We already know everything we need to know—we've simply forgotten. As we passed into the Earth plane of existence our awareness was erased or dulled. As children, we knew we were powerful and imagined our thoughts and wishes made things happen. Over time, we were convinced by well-meaning adults that we didn't have that power. This is one reason why we have to re-learn the basic creative principles of life.

Remember being a kid and having "imaginary friends?" Or knowing what was going to happen and being told you were crazy? One of the most important aspects of learning manifesting is remembering your intuitive and energetic power.

Another way we were convinced this power didn't exist was because we tried to make things happen and it didn't work out. We gave up. Although thoughts create reality, there is a definitely a safeguard of time between thought and manifestation. This gives us time to take it back. It also means our intentions must be specific and repeated in order to create results.

Can you imagine if everything you thought would create reality instantly? What a disaster!

When you think about the thoughts that spontaneously pop up in your mind on an hourly basis without obvious direction by you, you can imagine the disaster scenarios of having instantaneous manifestation. Most of us do not want that. Yet there is a strong tradition of spiritual and prosperity philosophy, now backed up by neurophysics and science, that teaches us our thoughts are constantly creating our reality. So gaining control of the mind is a crucial task for every one of us.

So, here we go. The Seven Steps of Manifestation.

Step One: State The Goal in Positive Language

Before we can create what we want, we have to actually know *what* we want. This might seem elementary, but it is an easily missed point. We may think we know, but often desires are framed in a sea of doubts or blockages. The thought and word messages we project are scrambled, ambivalent or downright contradictory. To empower intention, goals must be infused with spiritual authenticity and be clearly worded—both in our thoughts and in any words we speak about our goal.

Many unexamined goals have arisen to satisfy a need that speaks through an uncontrolled mind. The random thought generator mind creates things we believe will give us happiness, without ever exploring where happiness comes from or if these ideas will generate contentment at all. As I embarked on this process myself, I realized at one point that I was mindlessly manifesting things my mother liked, including her ideal house—decades after I'd left home.

Connection to soul purpose through astrology and meditative inner process is a preliminary step for Step One. As you clarify your soul purpose and intentions, remember that every aspect of life has both beautiful benefits and tragic challenges. Life holds all experiences equally, even if our human selves consider some things good and others bad.

Many years ago I was a single mother, wishing desperately to find a new partner. I sat by the stream at the Taos Pueblo and asked the Grandmother Spirit, "When will I find my true love?"

She replied to me: "*Enjoy the time you have now. Right now you have the problem of being alone. Soon you will have the problem of being in relationship.*"

THE MAGIC OF DETAILS:

At Step One of manifestation, it is important to focus on the details. Next we'll release the details and embrace the essence of the energetics, but first you need to consider exactly what you imagine you want and need. If you're going to create consciously, the Universe needs to understand fully and clearly what you're creating. And you need to align your desire nature with your true path so you're not wasting effort on mental tangents.

The container, or overview, takes you back to the soul level goals you identified in Chapter 3. In each of the twelve sections, relating thematically to the twelve houses of the chart, you wrote down what was working, and what wasn't.

1. Write down exactly what you wish to create under each one of these categories. Use precise numbers, dates, and details as much as you can. These details should be written in affirmation form, which means the positive tense, such as, "I have five new friends," or "I make $100,000 a year," or "I am vibrantly healthy." Negative words are not included in the way words and thoughts become form, so thoughts like, "I am no longer poor," or "I am not crazy," are changed by the universal manifesting machine into "I am poor," and "I am crazy." Honestly, I don't know why this amazingly complex world can't understand complex sentence structure but it does seem to be true. Clear, simple, positively-worded affirmations work best. As for the current tense issue, that's simple. We are always in a "now" moment. If you say, "I will be healthy," that implies you will be healthy in the future. From the now moment, the future is always out there somewhere. This truth is a little cagey to me too, because if all time exists at once, then using words of past, present or future are all irrelevant. But again, there is consensus that current-time language works best, and it is simple enough to do.

2. Double check to ponder if these goals actually align with your higher vision. Compare these goals with your Mission Statement.

3. Highlight the goals you believe are most important.

4. Note the goals that seem easy or quick to accomplish.

5. Break down the bigger goals into manageable subgoals.

6. Pick the one, most important goal on your list to use for the next steps. This goal, stated in positive current language, is your starting point for the following steps.

7. Once you're satisfied with your list, write the universal disclaimer on it. This is truly old-school but is very important: "This, or something greater, for the highest good of all concerned." Why? Because your ego mind is somewhat limited. You can put a lot of energy into creating things that aren't nearly as amazing as the perfection Spirit can serve up for you. And you want your goals to be for the highest good of everyone, not creating karma and problems you can't foresee. (The angelic legal team came up with this one).

8. Finally, make a copy of the list and fold it into eight (three folds) and place it on your altar or under a candle or crystal with the objective that these intentions go out into the cosmos to be created easily. The original is your working copy. Read it when you need a reminder of the awesome power of thought.

What if you're not sure about the specific goal?

Use the most specific aspects of the goal you can think of. For example, you don't like your current career and would like something different but are not sure what that is. If you're deciding whether you would want to be a therapist, coach or hypnotherapist and don't feel ready to say something like, "I am now a successful psychotherapist," you can say "I now have a successful career helping people."

Step Two: Discover the Underlying Essence of the Goal

Your goals are now specific, detailed and in the positive, current-moment tense. Your crystal is working overtime to magnify the intentions. You have harnessed the power of clear thought underwritten by soul path intentions.

Now consider the essence of the one goal you'd like to work with first. If your goal is financial, the underlying essence is that you want security. If you want to be married, what you actually want is love and maybe stability. Career goals often have to do with service, accomplishment, or a feeling of worth.

What is the essence of your goal?

Imagine you have accomplished the goal and you now feel the essential resulting emotion. Luxuriate in security, love, harmony, balance . . . whatever is the feeling essence you imagine will be accomplished. **Spend at least five minutes a day imagining the feeling you will have as if you have already achieved your goal.**

This imagination process connects the creative power of images with the magnetism of emotion. When you imagine how you will feel when you have accomplished something, you experience the actual feelings you're aiming for. Emotion draws experiences to you that are in alignment with the emotion.

Step Three: Discover and Shift Subconscious Blocks

Step Three works with the parts of you that hold objections against your goal. This is the often overlooked crucial step. Positive thought is powerful and rewires the brain to think along new and more creative pathways. Yet anyone who has worked with positive thought knows there are very powerful objecting negative voices and intractable feelings. These voices are stubborn and sneaky. They are capable of sabotaging even the most devoted expression of millions of positive thoughts.

Repeat your affirmation whenever you think of it until you can feel that it is, in fact, already there. Develop a sense of curiosity about when and how it will show up in physical life. Imagine your delight and surprise.

Now notice the objections that arise, the inner voices that say no, this is never going to happen, and their reasons. Some objections will subside with continued repetition of the positive affirmation. Others will remain stubborn, a voice of ongoing subconscious blocking energy. Once you have discovered the voice of the blocking energy, you can do a psychosynthesis process meditation to get to know more about it, just as we did in earlier chapters. This process is most easily done with someone guiding you, but you can do it yourself if you need to. The details are in the Reflection section at the end of the chapter.

Step Four: Feel Real Emotion

Emotion is a critical factor in manifestation. Some feelings sabotage creation, while others act as the magnetic force field to draw desired events toward you. Complex and confused feelings keep you swirling in circles. Attached feelings block manifestation. Nonattached feelings can scare us into thinking we won't create anything we truly want. And in fact, when we've completely detached, we often feel that we don't even want the cherished original outcome. We've changed our "mind."

Step Four asks that you develop contentment to allow the flow of creation to work through you effortlessly. Take some time to clear the emotional body and corresponding emotional chakras. Emotional clarity softens the habit pattern of striving against the plan of life and allows powerful acceptance.

You have contemplated the emotional essence of how you'd like to feel. *But what about how you actually feel?* It is empowering to feel feelings as they are without fighting against them or trying to change them. They will change spontaneously when we give them presence and space.

As you move through the day, allow feelings to move through you as much as you are able. Breathe into them. Most of us are afraid of strong feelings. We don't want to feel pain, anger and rage, so we only let little bits of them seep out. When we can't contain them any longer, we explode, creating havoc and discomfort, and possibly broken dishes.

If we move in the other direction to feel bliss and happiness, we are often afraid we will lose these more cherished feelings. Hoping to avoid future pain, we minimize the joy with the idea that we are "just setting ourselves up." We go up and down in this cycle—attach and contract.

Often we tell ourselves that painful memories are in the past and we need to just "move on and let go," minimizing the feelings and the long-range impact these events had on us. When we are not comfortable with emotion or we are unable to feel it, observe it and release it like the energy it is, our stuck, old feelings keep us prisoners of attachment, causing us to stay in unhealthy jobs and unhappy relationships.

It may be that when you try to visualize your desired emotional states, you can't actually feel them fully. When you conjure up feelings of security, bliss or love as your idea of how you'll feel when you attain your goal, you might feel frightened, discouraged or unlovable.

Feelings are energy. They are messengers, offering feedback about possible action. As we learn to feel all feelings without judgment, attachment or repulsion, they lose their grip. We become lighter and clearer. There is more space in our lives for soul-centered creation.

Step Five: Take Action

The Universe loves action. It is empowering to show up and take action in the physical. Just do it, as the saying goes. The healing work we can do in creative psychic space through positive thought, meditation and visualization is undoubtedly amazing. The majority of what is needed to shift energy and manifest remarkable results comes from positive thought and softening emotional habit pattern objections. It's possible to create some of our wishes just from the mental/emotional perspective in alignment with soul path.

Getting out there and doing something sure helps the cause. If nothing else, it gives us a concrete use for our energy and places us in situations where it's easier for the creative principles of the universe to provide. We meet people. We let people know we exist. Opportunities are offered. Physical space for our offerings are created.

The statement of manifestation is: "Physical reality is created through thought, word and **action**."

The Universe loves action.

Soul path goals are crystallized through intentional action.

What steps do you need to take to move toward this specific goal? Make a list if you want, but start taking action. Think of little tiny baby steps. You can crawl, even. Just show your goal that you care, that you mean it, and that you're showing up to create your intentions through action.

Step Six: Forgiveness & Gratitude

Forgiveness and gratitude are classic spiritual choices. They are attitudes and inspirations for the daily practice of life. Forgiveness and gratitude both dissolve stuck energy and open our hearts. They smooth out the creation process so that we receive blessings beyond the limited thoughts of imagination.

The words alone won't shatter resentments, pain, anger or selfishness. The words create an intention. With time and focus, you empower the intention. From the intention you will experience the truth of your feelings. Objections and blockages arise. Blame and guilt surface. Forgiveness and gratitude can be powerful allies and tools to uncover truth within until you truly forgive and are fully grateful.

When you *really* mean it, the Universe knows. Until then, "fake it till you make it" moves you in the right direction and provides insight into blocking energies.

FORGIVENESS

There are some experiences in life that are hard to forgive—maybe impossible. Some people seem too cruel to even think about forgiving. Oprah was going to write a book on the power of forgiveness—apparently actually did write it—and then she realized that people who had been abused in unspeakable ways would read it and might feel shamed and guilt-tripped into forgiving. So she decided not to publish it.

Yet all of our spiritual traditions ask us to forgive. We hear quippy slogans like, "Holding onto anger and resentment is like taking poison and expecting the other person to die." Pain and hatred sicken us. That is clear. Not forgiving gets in the way of love, contentment, of peaceful daily living. Yet forcing forgiveness feels non-empathic, insensitive, and perhaps not even possible.

In the process of manifestation I encourage you to *explore* forgiveness with an understanding that sooner or later, in this life or another, you will have to forgive everyone who has harmed you so you can release the experience from your energy field and stop repetitive karma. It's that simple. Wounds are like catnip to pain. The same or similar wounding experiences will find your unhealed traumas.

As you explore forgiveness, the feelings you actually feel must be given permission to arise and be seen. If you are able, you can feel them too, little by little, as you can handle them. Sometimes the well is deep and unbearable. You need time and a powerful yet gentle guide (therapist, good friend, beloved) to witness your pain and hold you as you allow it to emerge.

The intention to forgive is the choice to set yourself free. Forgiveness does not condone the harm that was done. Perhaps it makes sense to you to understand that as souls we are perfect and we are players in each other's movies. Your abusers and those who made your life difficult agreed to play this role in your life, as you have for others in this or other lives. You can have this belief, but you'll still have human feelings about it. Maybe this spiritual philosophy makes you want to scream and tear your hair out and you simply want to hate the people who harmed you. Feel that too. Forgiveness is a process and you get to start where you are. The layers include facing what happened and feeling the cornucopia of hard emotions, from anger and hopelessness to fears and inner doubts. And then, maybe, there's an understanding that helps make sense of it all.

When you have, perhaps over many years, felt what you need to feel, released the energy, releasing the story line . . . maybe you will arrive at a place of peace, contentment. Maybe it's a hurt that never totally goes away. The intention to forgive gradually morphs into real forgiveness and a freedom from the event. The wound is transmuted into power. This is the process of Pluto in astrology—fearless excavation of the many layers of wounding until true power and integrity have been cultivated in the ash of the nuclear blast that torched some area of your life. We all have something that left us burned to shreds.

As you consider the intention you are manifesting in this seven step process, consider whom (if anyone) you want to forgive for contributing to your wounding, your sense that others helped create the blockages that hold you back. Simply notice what arises, from, "I can never forgive that," to, "My intention is to forgive," to, "I have forgiven—there is no energy here anymore."

GRATITUDE

Gratitude is a little easier, but not so simple when we feel stuck and blocked, thinking we're years behind schedule.

Like forgiveness, the cousin of gratitude starts with mouthing the words.

Thank you. I am grateful for all that I have.

Do this in general, whenever you think of it. Or perhaps every day, if you have that kind of mind.

Expressing gratitude for what you want to create—even before it has magically appeared—is where gratitude flexes its muscle and becomes a magical tool.

Gratitude for what you have that you don't want, the stuff you want to kick to the curb: that's high-wizard craft.

So you want to be married and you haven't had a date for five years? Can you be thankful for the joys of being single? Can you be thankful for the mate you know is there but you haven't actually met yet? Can you be grateful for every single problem, every single blessing, in every moment that you remember to breathe and remember gratitude?

If you can do this, your life will blossom. Period.

Step Seven: Surrender & Let Go

Now kiss your goal goodbye. Imagine it as a butterfly that came to light on your hand. Kiss. Blow. Off it goes.

Stop thinking about it. Trust that it's in the works. You've done everything you need to do. You will, just to be sure, continue to think positively about it showing up at any minute on your doorstep, and you will join Match.com, get an advanced physics degree, buy a dog or take a trip to Jamaica. But apart from that, you will stop stressing about what isn't happening, and only place your energy on what is happening in your life in this current moment, right in front of you, with the full awareness and trust that whatever you have worked on manifesting is in process of being delivered.

This, or something better, for the highest good of all concerned.

This statement takes you off the hook from your limited ego/mind creating something inferior to what is actually in store for you by the abundant Universe. (*By the way: What is the Universe? Simply the sum total of all energy of which we are all One. That's why each one of us getting clear helps everyone else on Earth. We are the Universe either giving lustrously or blocking endlessly, usually both at the same time.*)

Surrender can be challenging, because we often imagine that to surrender means we give up control and the tight grip we hold on our life and goals. Then we tell ourselves that means we will lose the power to create, all will be lost and nothing created. Exactly wrong. We hold on too tightly to our desires and goals. We forget (or don't know) that grasping stops or slows the progress of manifestation.

We also forget, our goals and aims may not be nearly as magnificent as what is in store for us. Our limited ego/minds want to create an affordable house in Akron and a roadworthy car. Meanwhile, our Spirit plans that we journey to Guatemala to help orphans, where we will meet our best soul mate friends and begin an adventurous new life that ultimately includes an even better home and fantastic wheels.

Through your very best contemplation, inner exploration and outer research, you are still working through the limited filter of your human ego/mind. Open up to what you don't know. Let go of control. Surrender and trust the outcome.

How many steps to manifest a mansion? Seven steps.

Like hopscotch, repeated again and again, perhaps skipping a step here and there because a stone is in the way, yet repeated quickly and nimbly until the actions are natural, easeful and automatic.

If you've been paying attention along the way you're probably not sure a mansion is in your highest and best interests, a worthy goal of an awesome soul path.

So now . . . What do you want? Who are you?

P.S.: Did you notice the steps are an exercise in the Four Pillars of Healing: spiritual overview of soul path to choose manifestation goals, mental process and review, emotional healing and presence, physical action, back to spiritual principles. Life principles are somewhat repetitive. Once you've figured out the system and work with each pillar, it's always more of the same.

REFLECTION #15

Soul Path Offering: The Seven Creation Steps

Use your Mission Statement and subgoals as the basis for these exercises

1. **Define a goal** based on your soul path awareness. State the goal specifically as a positive affirmation in current time. "I now am/have _____."
2. Discover the **underlying essence** of the goal in terms of how you imagine feeling once you have created it. Revel in the feelings.
3. Discover and heal the **subconscious thought blockages** that resist your goal (Reflection processes follow).
4. **Feel all of your feelings** without resistance.
5. **Take actions** in the physical reality toward your goal.
6. Cultivate **forgiveness and gratitude** related to your goal (and everything in your life, just for good measure).
7. **Surrender and trust** that this or something better in accordance with divine creation is in process. Relax and let go.

Repeat these seven steps with each goal. It's best to focus on one goal at a time, although the others may be "simmering" in the background with your manifestation list.

2. Meditation #15.1 - Meditation for the Resistant Subpersonality

You have noticed that every time you say your affirmation, you hear a strong oppositional voice. This meditation will be to get to know the "Resistance Part" of you.

Get into a comfortable, relaxed position and slow your breath. Close your eyes. Make sure distractions are turned off and you have some time. You can find your best time of day, a relaxing bath, or perfect peaceful location.

Imagine you are in nature in a peaceful setting. Allow the part of you that speaks this "no" voice to show up; the part of you that resists your affirmation. You will see it or feel it like it is a person, cartoon figure or shape of energy. Allow a picture to float up in your mind. Spend some time looking at the picture, feeling its emotional energy or attitude, and getting to know more about it. You might wonder how long it has been with you, or if it resists other intentions in your life. Imagine you're having a conversation with this part of you like it's a person you've just met.

You can then ask it why it's blocking you. More specifically, what does it truly need? You can see here that this part is a bit like exploring essential needs. You can then offer to give this part what it needs, or imagine calling that need in as an energy form. If it needs love, imagine a warm, soft loving energy, enveloping this part. If it needs security, perhaps you can think of an image that surrounds this part and allows it to feel secure. Your intuitive imagination will come up with perfect images for you and your parts.

If this part is very angry, dark or menacing and refuses to receive healing, call in the Archangel Michael and Angels of Light to surround it with Light. And then get some help from someone who works with energetic healing. Some blocking energies are very forceful and hard to work with alone.

When you feel you have provided enough energy to the part (this is a subjective, intuitive feeling that it is "enough"), leave it bathing in the energy and move to the blockage.

3. Meditation #15.2: Meditation to Release Emotional Blockage to Your Goal

In step #4, you allowed yourself to feel your feelings— all of them. If there is a blocking emotion you'd like to soften, this meditation allows you to explore it. Based on self-hypnosis, spiritual inquiry, and the Focusing work of Eugene Gendlin, this meditation teaches us that being with an emotion we generally resist tends to soften and destabilize it rather quickly.

Think now of that feeling.

Place yourself in a comfortable position, close your eyes, and breathe deeply and slowly. You might imagine a beautiful color of healing light and/or that you're in a beautiful place in nature, safe and secure.

As you continue to hold the one word that describes your blocking emotion in your mind, the word that describes that feeling, breathe gently and notice where in your body you are holding the energy of that feeling. Breathe into that area, simply watching and noticing if there are any changes, without trying to force changes. Just observe.

As you breathe into the area, you might find that the word in your mind changes. A new word may arise. It may be a phrase. Using that word or phrase, continue breathing into the part of the body that feels contracted or holding with the energy. You may feel a sensation of softening or release. The word may change more than once.

It's okay if nothing changes. Stay with the breath.

If you are visual, notice the color and shape of the emotion. Does it have smooth or rough edges? Are you willing to release it? Is it willing to go? How long has it been there? Does it imagine it is helping or hindering you? You can call in healing guides to help with this part.

Energy can also be released by a meditation to burn it out with imaginary violet flame, doing a psychic surgery to cut it out, melting it so it blows away on a breeze or pours out like liquid. Whichever way you choose, send the dark energy to the cosmos, a mountaintop or to the ocean, or some other transformative place where it will be purified.

Fill yourself with healing light from the cosmos, the Earth, and/or your high Spirit energy.

3. Soul Path Offering: Burn & Release

Another old magical technique for releasing emotion is to write the difficult experiences and challenging feelings on a piece of paper that you'd like to release. Burn the piece of paper with the intention that you are releasing the feelings and the karma. This is particularly good to do on a full moon day. *(Please burn safely. I like to burn things in a metal bowl set in the sink. A fireplace would work, or an outdoor fire pit.)*

You can do these exercises with unprocessed emotional energies you are carrying, or feelings you have absorbed from others, but you cannot release your inner parts. Your inner parts make up who you are and it is best to get to know them. You can give them what they need and find ways to use their gifts and skills while negotiating with them to minimize the ways they block you.

4. Meditation #15.2: Forgiveness

Begin by breathing slowly as you arrive in gentle meditation. Imagine you're in a huge grassy field or on a wide open beach. Everyone you've ever known in this life is standing there opposite you—perhaps hundreds of people. In your mind, you say to them, with as much truth and feeling as you can cultivate:

"I now forgive you for all the ways you have harmed me, in this life and all others."

"I now ask you to forgive me for all the ways I have harmed you, in this life and all others."

"I now forgive myself for all the ways I have harmed myself and all sentient beings, in connection with this karma, in this life and all others."

Most likely most of them will dissolve, fade away, or move back. They are the ones where the karma is minimal or already complete. There may be a couple of people who stand firm, or move closer. Maybe you've even forgotten about one of them. You may then need to do this meditation again, more than once, with the remaining individuals, one by one. Take your time. This is true magic.

Part Five

LIVING THE SOUL PATH WAY

CHAPTER SIXTEEN

The Daily Plan

"Freedom is not given to us by anyone;
we have to cultivate it ourselves.
It is a daily practice."
—Thich Nhat Hanh

At this point, you've been examining your life from every direction. Feelings, thoughts and ideas may have emerged, ranging from exciting epiphanies to overwhelming life projects looming like swirling galaxies in front of you. How can you accomplish your soul path when life itself seems to take up every waking moment and somehow you know you need more hours for sleep too? Has anyone invented the thirty-two-hour day yet?

A good daily plan includes a balance of disciplined action and the flexibility to choose intuitively. Rigid discipline with endless tasks, even toward the illustrious goal of soul intention, weighs heavy. This is not about generating a dry, productive yet soulless life, with a strict to-do list that stifles your life force. Circling around in a morass of feelings, waiting for the urge to do something, tends to be ungrounded and unproductive; nothing gets done.

When you map an intentional day, you create a bit more focus, a possibility of balance. When the plan doesn't feel balanced, you can make a slight adjustment and settle in to a different feel. Structure and intuitive wisdom find their rightful place. From time to time, if you find yourself overwhelmed with too much to do, you can afford to drop a nonessential activity off the list for a day. Three hours previously accounted for are now yours to play with: Voila! Instant mini-vacation. Small changes generate space or struggle. You get to feel in and decide.

Your priorities are unique to you. They will change with the seasons, with cycles of life.

We sometimes get stuck in ideas about life and choices without taking the time to stop and think creatively. I remember how I transitioned from going to the gym for cardio and weight workouts to adding one yoga class a week at the gym. Then two. Then I discovered Forrest Yoga and added that class at a yoga studio once a week. At the time, it was kind of a radical idea to go to yoga classes three times a week. For most of my life, if I took yoga classes, I always went once a week. I have no idea why.

You can substitute the word "yoga" with anything else you do occasionally or regularly. How did you decide how often you would do it? What happens to your life balance when you decide to do something more or less?

I overheard a student tell my yoga teacher how he was improving and feeling so much better since he started taking classes twice a week. For some reason, this amazed me. I hadn't thought I could do this intense yoga more than once a week. So I changed my schedule around so I could go twice a week too, and indeed made progress.

Months later, I was sitting in class next to Alex, who told me she went to five classes a week and couldn't function without them. Wow! I found this stunning at the time. This busy mother who owned her own business took ninety minutes every day to come to this powerfully intense yoga class. Soon I was there five and six days a week too, changing all my bodies—emotional, mental, physical and spiritual—rapidly.

Next level of change: After years of the intensity of almost daily vigorous practice, my yoga mentor suggested I develop a shorter morning home practice and take fewer public classes, at least until the book was written. Another inner shift occurred. It can take a lot of intention to get to bed early enough to get up early enough to have a morning practice. It's so easy to make a cup of coffee or tea, open up the computer and whoosh . . . the morning is g.o.n.e.

And then there's evening time. Tired, drained . . . the lure of the zone-out screens. It's so easy to watch TV or catch up on email or Facebook, even though we know now that the blue screen light affects melatonin and our sleep cycle. And the research gets clearer by the day that getting enough sleep is an important factor in all facets of health.

Between dawn and dusk we are drawn to various activities that may or may not be aligned with our path. Why do we do them? Often we are drawn into other people's needs and agendas. It can be hard to say no to invitations. We have deeply embedded ideas about how clean the house should be, how much time we should devote to cooking, the kids, pet walking . . . life is a full-time job.

In the Reflection section, you will create your own daily plan in alignment with your intentions. This is conscious life in action. You take the time to consider who you are and why you're here. You do this without judgment or harshness, but hopefully with the compassion and empathy for yourself you would give to others. You set the steps and mini-goals. You hold these goals in a container of spiritual acceptance that everything is perfect as it is. Simple steps set up a life where it is possible and even flowing to manifest your dreams. Otherwise you'll be on your deathbed wondering where your life swept away to.

To center your life in conscious activity from morning until night, consider these juicy possibilities.

MORNING

- Wake up and look out the window at the sky. The light helps the brain wake up
- Endeavor to accept the day with grace and gratitude. Check the mind's tendency to judge the day or the weather "good" or "bad" for some reason.
- Wash your face with cool water.
- Massage your body with warm oil or lotion, before or after your shower.
- Drink a mug of warm water with lemon, or even a large glass of room temperature water, to allow the body to complete the elimination of toxins from its night activities.
- Morning meditation: Spend at least five to ten minutes sitting in breath meditation. If you don't have an altar and a comfortable place to meditate, look around to find a corner somewhere in your home to create a sacred space. An altar can be any table or small box, even, with a few things on it that feel special to you: a candle, incense, a picture of a beloved teacher, a little statue, crystals and stones, feathers. You decide what items connect you to your heart.
- Do some morning yoga or stretching.
- Read or remember your soul path mission statement and set an intention for the day.

There's more you can add: Ayurvedic morning rituals for your particular type, extra yoga, chanting, breathing or exercise. Maybe part of your morning is taking the dog for a walk, or making a hot mug of tea. Perhaps you have children pulling at your toes before you even wake up and the morning ritual is a big full breath as you look out the window and raise your arms over your head . . . and then—showtime. It's on. Whatever you choose, keep in mind that the purpose of the morning ritual is to remember you're a Spirit having a physical experience *before* the ducks of life start pecking at you, drawing you into story and reaction.

DURING THE DAY

- Take small, mindful actions toward your goals. Break your goals into mini-goals. Allow fifteen minutes to be a worthy step.

- Organize your living space. Release clutter and unneeded items.

- Take a savasana restorative nap or just rest. Think of how you lie down and do nothing on a vacation and how good that feels (or maybe you have heard of someone who once rested while on vacation).

- Dance and sing.

- Slow down and drive the speed limit. Let other cars go in front of you.

- Make eye contact with people. Smile.

- Get outside with your bare feet in the grass whenever you can.

EVENING

- Consider a limited TV/media diet. What do you watch? How much life energy is it sapping?

- Choose a bedtime that allows you at least eight hours of sleep.

- Minimize screen time at least a couple of hours before bedtime.

- Eat your last meal hours before bedtime.

- Take a soothing bath.

- Read inspirational, healing or funny material before bed.

- Repeat a mantra as you fall asleep. I like "I am love," but it can be any word or sentence that feels nourishing to you.

Consider the cultivation of your daily life plan to be a gift to yourself—a gift that gives you balance and the sense that, despite the pushes and pulls of human life, you are making room for your sweetest dreams.

#16 - REFLECTION

1. Journal Reflection: Your Unique Daily Plan

Evaluate your daily life from the moment you wake up until bedtime. In order to add the activities and goals you've identified from the previous lessons as soul path, you might need to let go of other activities. This is challenging when you have small children, busy jobs and other responsibilities. Just imagine you were looking at someone else's life. What would you suggest releasing? Where is the wasted time?

If you want to be amazingly diligent, you can keep a time diary for a week or two and include other aspects of life you might want to track. The food you eat, the money you spend and the emotions that come as you make choices can make for a full and interesting exploration.

Whether you do a quick analysis or take time to keep a diary is up to you. As you see how you can release nonessential activities, begin to place soul-centered ones in the newly available time slots.

Transformation, an hour at a time.

CHAPTER SEVENTEEN

Beloveds & Tribe

*"As we let our light shine, we unconsciously give
other people permission to do the same.
As we are liberated from our own fear, our
presence actually liberates others."*
—Marianne Williamson

L ife can feel very lonely—or maybe that's just me. Even in the midst of family and friends, co-workers and community, there is an interesting dance between feeling supported and connected and the sense of a solitary path. For some, this is a definite, regular feeling: I am alone. I am lonely. For others, the sense of community, support and love nourishes and sustains, so the feeling of aloneness occurs less often and more fleetingly.

This sense of aloneness is amplified when we place a high value on connection with other humans, who may simply not be able to come through for us all of the time in the ways we desire.

Your issues and the other's issues collide. Just at the moment you wish for total unconditional support, your beloved may be having a bad day, feeling engulfed, needing space, kayaking in the wilds of Peru. The love and support of other humans is amazing and fulfilling, but it is not always reliable.

The reliable cure for a feeling of aloneness in the world is a strong sense of connection to Spirit. In that deep, quiet place within, we are connected to who we truly are, and that part of us is absolutely connected to all sentient life 100 percent of the time. Here, there are no bad moods or distant vacations.

The cultivation of connection at this level is achieved through meditation practice. Hopefully you've found a way to include meditation in your daily plan in a way that works for you, especially meditation that includes connecting to a sense of spirit permeating within and around you.

As you deepen your spiritual connection and awaken, even a little, step by step, you will reap huge benefits. Yet also your regular life relationships will be tested. When you step onto the spiritual, healing path, there's no certainty that your love and social relationships will survive. You may need to be courageous and feel socially alone for a while until your new tribe and beloveds show up. You can speed up the process and go looking for the new tribe, but sometimes when you're in transition, you're actually not in the mood for socialization. Or, you aren't sure exactly who the next cohorts are.

Do you remember when you first understood alternative concepts and said yes to the path of the seeker? Was it a radical change, or did it look like a series of small nods and steps toward conscious life?

As I said, I had an immediate visceral "truth" reaction to first hearing about reincarnation. *This is true.* Then I heard about spirit guides. Big "yes" within my body, a felt sense of truth again. I still didn't understand the nature of my own psychic powers, but I had always listened to (though not always followed) this voice in my head. I had known unknowable details since I was a small child. Like many psychics, I went through early dark years, self-destructive and alone, always feeling like an outsider and an impostor. I didn't believe in God at the time because I cringed at the hypocrisy of organized religion—at least as I'd experienced it growing up. Many years passed before I was ready to open my heart, read the metaphysical books that had piled up beside the bed, and ultimately find a teacher and some classes.

Then came the family challenge, verbalized by my mom. "You don't believe in that psychic BS do you?" she demanded as she noticed *The Psychic Healing Handbook* on my kitchen table. "You've never been normal!" It took years for her to come around and appreciate my gifts and life calling. I was already the family black sheep. My spiritual and metaphysical pursuits widened the chasm between me and my family.

Friends—I lost most of them. I'd been in the corporate world trying to be "not sensitive," as a result of the brilliant plan I'd hatched in my early twenties. I imagined that accountants were not the most sensitive types, and everyone had always told me I was too sensitive. Therefore, I decided to become an accountant. From those studies, I went to night school to earn an MBA in Finance. Now in my gray Brooks Brothers suit and white button-down shirt, I was definitely playing the part of "not sensitive." And a complete mess inside.

I also harbored a secret life of interest in alternative healing. Macrobiotics, shiatsu and other healing pursuits kept me healthy despite other self-destructive choices. The transition occurred in a bridge year when I set up a business (old world) to market high-end supplements to alternative doctors (new world). Technically this year was a failure. The business deal I'd taken was guaranteed to fail; I lost all my money. Yet even then, I could see the failure year had set me on a new path. I met people who had given up their lucrative medical practices to provide holistic medicine. Each one had a particular alternative philosophy. They held various spiritual beliefs from Buddhist to Christian and everything in between that fueled their integrity. At the end of the year, the old life had burned off and I was fully engaged with the new path.

Psychotherapy, meditation, crystal workshops, tarot, a psychic healer guide . . . once I stepped on that path it was an escalator, one direction and moving fast. In my new life as a psychic and healer, a whole new world opened in front of me as the old world vanished. I met new friends; a new social circle emerged.

Not everyone makes a swift transition. And not everyone lives in California or a liberal coastal enclave. You might be awakening in the outback of conservative territory. The risk of letting people know what you actually believe and how you're trying to open up to consciousness can feel profoundly scary.

If you are living a life that looks "regular" from the outside, exploring healing and spirituality, carefully sharing only with a few friends, no doubt you will feel isolated. Even more challenging is when you cannot share your spiritual or healing path with a mate for fear you are leaving them behind, or a family you know rejects your beliefs. These fears are not ungrounded. It happens. You can definitely evolve yourself to the point you feel even more alone than you did when trying to pretend to be normal. It becomes harder and harder to talk at family events. If you show up wearing a crystal, or mention a workshop you've taken, you might experience teasing and flat-out shaming.

There's no easy solution. You'll find yourself balancing prior commitments and connections with the need to find your more aligned tribe. Most of us do need support from other humans. Friendship and love fill our hearts and make life bearable in the more challenging moments. Even within the realm of spiritual seekers or metaphysical believers, you still need to find the specific soul family with which you feel aligned. This can take time and patience. Then, as you continue to open your heart, you might also find that you feel more and more comfortable with everyone. The rigidity of preference and judgment dissolves.

You can find your tribe at workshops and classes and various spiritual events. Listen to your gut intuition and go to the events that appeal to you. Once there, feel the vibe from the speaker/s and from the folks around you.

The complexity of the path is evident in a hot, sweaty yoga class of one hundred or more bodies. There is a feeling of being in this thing together, yet also in our own process. We are guided by teachers, held in community, but the minute the class is over students rush to the cubbies to get their stuff and back out to the driven life. It might take arriving a bit early or hanging around afterward drinking tea to get to know someone. From alone to group connection to a sip of tea, maybe a connection outside of the event. Savvy studios and teachers encourage connection through their events.

As we traverse the next decades, community will become increasingly important. The Internet, chat rooms, Facebook and other technological breakthroughs give us the means to connect with everyone, a vast cyber friend world. But like the rush out the door after a live event, it takes action to create a real, in person friendship to truly fill our personal needs.

In a study on happiness and friendship by John F. Helliwell and Haifang Huang in 2013, the authors concluded that the more real, personal friends you have, the happier you are. In fact, doubling your number of friends in real life makes you as happy in real life it makes you as happy as if you had a 50 percent increase in income. As we would suspect, friends were more important for single people who were not married or partnered. Statistically, the number of online friends you have doesn't affect happiness at all. Converting the online friends you resonate with to an in-the-flesh, face-to-face friend is crucial for creating a soul-nurturing tribe.

In your assessment of the twelve areas of life, you contemplated friends, partnerships and other relationship aspects of your life. What are your personal unique goals and intentions?

Regardless of whether you thought you wanted more people in your life, there can be value in creating life through tribe. We are connected in an interwoven fabric of life. What you believe and think about the people around you affects them. And vice versa. Your friends' and relatives' thoughts and opinions about you are constantly adding to the creation power—or decreasing the power—available to you.

Let me repeat that in a different way. If your friends or family put you down, make fun of you, don't understand why you're into that "psychic BS," think you're crazy to decide to ditch your life-sucking job for creative or healing pursuits that call to you, their energy is draining you. You will need to work extra hard to shield yourself from their negative, draining energies, or, sadly, you will need to step away from them.

On the other hand, there are numerous benefits to reaching out for your true and aligned tribe. There can be joy and amplifying power when you find even a few people in your tribe who can help in the evolutionary and manifesting/co-creative process.

When you reach out to the friends who are on the same path as you and invite them to support you in your goals, you are able to create and manifest more powerfully. You can offer your support to them too.

Together in ever-expanding circles of intent we may even be able to shift the world. There is a tipping point energetically when what was once an outrageous thought becomes commonplace. "Crazy" turns into struggle and then suddenly becomes "of course." We've seen this recently in terms of gay marriage rights and the movement to legalize marijuana.

Before you unfriend virtually everyone on Facebook and send good-bye emails to everyone else, stop and consider this opposing view that adds complexity and nuance to everything I've just said.

Accept the relationships you're in, right now, fully. Take responsibility for every one of them having been perfect and your choice. This is an important step in healing. Everyone in your life is your teacher. You are their teacher. As you take a step back to look at what you've been learning, acceptance and truth can be the key to the exit door, if that's where you're headed. And sometimes you don't have to leave when you're whole within yourself.

Culturally we have a lot of emphasis on receiving, setting boundaries, and what is working for "us." Set some intention to give to others however and whenever you can. The heart/mind quality of devotion can be a powerful healing tool in all of your relationships. Even though it might seem counterintuitive to practice devotion toward someone who is aggressively negative or hurtful to you, the power of devotion coming from a true heart perspective includes devotion to yourself, the other, and to Spirit. In this context, devotion might help you get unstuck.

Belinda was in a difficult relationship with a man who seemed to love her in some ways, but criticized her and wasn't always honest. She decided to devote herself to the relationship while also devoting herself to her own life plan, choosing not to continue agonizing about his behavior or trying to change him, which hadn't been working anyway. She had tried to leave him numerous times; every time they had reconciled. Leaving hadn't worked. Staying and being in pain didn't work. Devotion was a last possibility. She simply decided to love him as he was and to accept the relationship. She felt deep peace in this decision. Her heart remained open, without expectation of change. Two months later, he ended the relationship unexpectedly and with a sense of certainty. Both of them felt fully complete and resolved. They didn't get back together.

Why would this happen? Again, you can think of people as "players in your movie." Your soul plan calls for a little vignette film. Best soul friends sign up to play the parts. Each part is actually an aspect of you, separated out and acted out. You can get mad at them for playing the part, or you can take responsibility for this being your lesson and consider what you're learning and what the most evolved action is for you now. When you choose the attitude of devotion to the reality of your current situation, you bring love and nonresistance to the reality. Old patterns may more easily melt. Love heals; devotion is a tendril of love.

There will also be relationships in your life you feel you can't end. Certain family members, exes with whom you've had children, friends you feel a strong connection with even though they're not heading along the same path . . . Life is complex.

Hold these relationships with as much unconditional love, devotion and acceptance as you can cultivate. Attitude is always a choice. Hold your boundaries too. You don't have to accept criticism and abuse. Remember the section on energetic boundaries and visualize strong light and boundaries around you when you need to interact with people who attack. You can also hold a stance of love and acceptance that permeates you so strongly that the critical is vanquished in a magical way.

Many years ago when my special-needs son was in school, I was to attend an IEP (independent education plan) meeting with the principal, teachers and various therapists who worked with him. I knew they wanted him to have a communication box and were planning to press their case at the meeting. At the time this box was much bigger than a laptop and had squares with images on it. For example, if he pressed a picture of an apple, the box would say "I want to eat please." This is a great invention for children who cannot talk, but I felt my son was making huge strides toward communication, and my intuition was that if he had this box, he would revert to this approach and stop trying to talk. This box would make it easier for his teachers but I didn't feel intuitively it was right for him at the time. As I sat in the car outside the school office, I connected in meditation with my high Self and the high Self of my son. I asked that the meeting go smoothly and in alignment with his highest path. I walked in the door of the meeting feeling loved and protected.

The meeting flowed like a charmed river. Everyone was in agreement. The speech therapist mentioned the box as a possibility but did not press the issue. The meeting moved on and everyone happily signed the documents for the year ... sans box.

Only the next day, the spell broke. The principal called me in a panic. "We were supposed to talk more about the communication box," she explained. But it was too late. The documents were signed and I didn't want to have them changed. By the next year he was talking well enough that it never came up again. This was a beautiful example of high, loving intentional energy shifting the words and actions of other people without conflict.

Manifesting Circles

Thought forms from both Spirit and ego consciousness create reality. Creation is not an individual process. We are not operating in a vacuum of our own little mind thoughts. Everyone's thoughts create everyone's reality.

The people we are most connected to may have thoughts about us and our plans that impact our creative power strongly. If our mates, family and friends think we're on the wrong path and don't trust our direction, we've got some hard work ahead to create a different life. If people truly "see" us and support us unconditionally, that supportive energy feeds us power.

Find a group of people who believe in you and provide positive energy for your intentions. This simple act of creating a "manifesting circle" can empower your healing and creative process. The circle can be specific: you can choose a group and decide to meet in person or online to state goals and have everyone send positive energy to your goal.

You can also choose to keep your intentions to yourself and only share with people you know will totally support you. This more subtle, undefined manifesting circle keeps your plans from being diluted by the nonbelievers.

In summary, you are not living in isolation energetically. The people with whom you surround yourself are part of your creation and manifesting process. As you evolve and grow, you will naturally want to be surrounded by more people who see you, accept you and support your spiritual path. It may take some time and direct action to create a new circle, yet once you have found your tribe and developed some close and loving relationships, you will find this supportive climate fosters a juicy manifesting energy to assist you in creating all you wish for.

#17 - REFLECTION

1. Journal Reflection: Beloveds & Tribe

Draw on your previous assessment of relationship in your life in all areas to reconsider the following types of relationships:

- *Family*
- *Children or pets*
- *Romance or fun friends*
- *Partner/s and committed friends*
- *Intimate, deep relationships*
- *Tribe or friends who share tasks or values in the world*

Feel into your sense of harmony and satisfaction with the people or beings in each area. Consider whether you'd like more, less or different relationships.

2. Meditation #17: Circle of Hearts

Place your body in a comfortable position and deepen your breath. As you breathe, imagine you are gently rising up into the cosmos, surrounded by stars and light. In this place, imagine you are sitting inside of a heart within a beautiful circle of hearts. In each heart, visualize a person who is dear to you and with whom you wish to maintain a close and loving relationship. Leave some hearts open and identify the type or quality of person you wish to show up to fill those hearts. You may wish for a partner, several new friends, a new nurturing person, a new therapist . . . any type of person or role. As you look to the side, notice or create a circle of hearts that represents people in your life with whom you desire less contact, even though you may have a life reason for your connection with them. These are the people who are critical or judgmental, who drain your energy. Place them in the circle of hearts and allow that circle to drift away to a distance where you feel some space. Breathe into your heart and infuse your love energy into each circle.

When you are finished, list in your journal the people you placed in your inner heart circle and also name the open places where you wish to call in new people as part of your inner heart circle.

3. Soul Path Offering: Manifesting Circle

Create a manifesting circle with a few of your close friends. This can be done either in person, or remotely through writing.

In person or via webinar or teleconferencing, invite each person to share their goal in positive present-tense language. After one person shares, have everyone send loving, supportive, powerful energy toward them and their goal for thirty to sixty seconds. Each person in the group should generally and regularly think of the person and goals with positive, strong support, *as if the goals are already manifested.*

The process is the same in writing: each person will share goals by email with all goals is mailed to everyone. A meditation time to connect to the goals can be set for everyone, or each person can send energy to the goal at whatever time works for them. Or, each person can agree to send power to the groups' goals every day for a number of days. Three, nine or thirty days are all good strong numbers for creativity.

CHAPTER EIGHTEEN

Connection to the World

"We can never obtain peace in the outer world
until we make peace with ourselves."
—Dalai Lama

If your email account is anything like mine, you could sit and watch the screen all day as the unsolicited letters flood in. This politician needs five dollars, that group needs $325,000 in the next twenty-four hours or else the other side will win and catastrophe will ensue. Buy handmade incense to support Tibetan nuns. The list goes on. There are news reports of the world going to hell faster than a handbasket could ever carry it.

The endless requests and perpetual bad news can be overwhelming. After the Paris bombings, several people told me they wanted to stop reading news altogether, to shut it all out. If you're an energetically sensitive person, a "media diet" can be a healing choice. Limit your exposure to news—especially visual news, which penetrates rapidly into the subconscious. The twenty-four-hour news stations are designed to keep you riveted to each unfolding disaster. Their broadcasts are repetitive and unnecessary, and feed into the addictive part of our brains. Yet to simply turn off completely and hide under the covers does not honor our soul connection with all beings. If we are completely out of touch, our ability to discern where we are drawn to be part of the solution is diminished.

Discernment is a crucial quality in this time of news noise, of desperate need for healing and change calling us from every direction. If you feel called, consider what your specific role might be. You cannot possibly align with every world cause, just as it's not required that each of us gets married or has a compelling career. You have a mix of choice and fated inner alignment with life experiences, whether they are countries or children, kitties or polar bears. Are you listening to your intuition about the level of engagement asked of you? Are you clear about your piece of the puzzle in the game of planetary transformation?

Your task is to find your unique connection to the greater world, take care of your nervous system (those who care tend to be extra sensitive), and find balance. You get to balance how you think and feel about world issues with your level of calling or connection and the tangible actions you might take.

You are a unique individual, yet you are not separate at all. Every single one of us, every animal, fish, bird, rock, and drop of water is infused with the same spirit. We are separate *and* connected. One and whole.

We can never completely disconnect ourselves from what is going on around us. We feel everything. There is a collective vibration of stress and suffering, joy and potential, flowing like a river beneath the surface of daily life. The Dalai Lama's quote above resonates. We can strategize to change the world or fight for peace, but true peace comes from within. If every human was brought up with humanitarian values and taught how to create the conditions for inner peace, we wouldn't have to wrestle with the endless wars and inequities. Solutions would be obvious. Action would be aligned with core values.

To achieve world peace, make peace within yourself. Be peace. Cultivate clarity. We have essential oneness with the world and every being in it, so your inner harmony creates a shift within the entire world.

Do not trivialize the contributions and chosen responsibilities that seem typical or "not enough." You can raise healthy children, offer any kind of work in the world that is carried out with integrity, or simply be of service when you are able. If a necessary requirement for world peace and justice is that each individual achieves peace within, then there are a myriad of activities and service possibilities that qualify as service to the greater world.

There will be some who are born to serve in grander ways on the world stage. If that's you, you already know that. Some of your healing work may be to risk greatness, to release fear of failure, and to jump in.

In addition, your connection to the world and your contribution to healing and change will be different at various life phases. In youth, we are often furious with hypocrisy and injustice and direct our vision and energy into highly visible activism. Marches and demonstrations, plus active volunteering, can be useful at this stage to effect change. Life purpose may morph into the creation and maintenance of a family (however we define family) and earning a living. Perhaps our contributions become harder to see unless we happen to be a healer or change-maker. As the dust settles and we phase out of the striving phase of life, there may be room again for more direct service in the world. Whatever phase of life you are in, a conscious awareness of your unique contributions will feed your sense of soul-centered connection.

Perhaps it doesn't matter so much *what* you do as *how* you engage with life.

You can choose whether or not you want to give money to the person begging for spare change at the street corner. How is your ego structure creating the story line? You may be in mental judgment and separation, ego elevation, or find this moment an opportunity to stay tuned to connection to all. Are you creating a story about how this person is different, lazy, going to use the money for drugs, should be working? Or do you feel superior because you have cash in hand as you bustle about your important activities? No, you are both exactly the same at the core. You are just at different phases—a different path, a different mock-up and manifestation based on prior-life experiences. The long-haired young man looking for spare change, with his guitar over his ragged shoulder and dog lying at his feet, may be a very evolved spirit, finding his way through a challenging life. We forget that most of us are a few paychecks away from homelessness, an earthquake away from devastation. Life is precarious. We turn away from the truth as we see the mirror shone toward us by our fellow travelers.

We are challenged on a daily basis to find balance and equanimity in all of our interactions with many people who are not coming from a peaceful place. Can you treat these frantic, stressed out beings with respect? Can you calm down and treat yourself with compassion when you're stressed? Can you see the divine in each face, allowing people to race in front of you in the grocery store, veer into your lane without signaling, serve up your latte with a sneer? As we deal with the world and our intention to maintain peace internally, we learn not to take aggressions personally, finding the breath and heart to see and feel without strong reaction.

You can react. There are moments for words. You don't have to be a whipping boy or victim to everyone's bad mood. But how often do we hold on to negative experiences, hours later still recounting the story of how someone cut us off in traffic, or angrily flopped our dinner plate onto the table. We need to become aware of overreaction, the duality of me versus you. Endless thinking about transgressions takes us off our path and into unbalanced ego land.

In the reflection section that follows, I ask you to create a list of what you do to help the world and what you'd like to do. I then ask you to repeat the affirmation: "I am enough. I do enough," with a loving, compassionate heart and notice what comes up. As always, the soul path is nuanced to the point of strongly oppositional force fields.

How can you do more?

How can you accept that what you're doing is enough?

This is the balance point of conscious reflection, to be willing to fearlessly see what you do (saving spiders and putting them outside), what you don't do (I know I need to slow down and drive the speed limit on the way to yoga), what calls to you (raising organic veggies), what you'd like to let go of (sending money to X organization just isn't cutting it anymore), what you'd like to do (a mural-making retreat to Peru sounds divine).

Just see it all. Feel it. And then be sure to surround the whole process with the underlying spiritual truth of life. You don't have to *do* anything. You are already perfect. The world is actually perfect and has carried on for millennia and will continue to do so. Let go of feeling overwhelmed and soul-sickeningly sad about how terrible everything is. Our love and acceptance is our greatest healing gift to ourselves and to the world.

#18 - REFLECTION

1. Meditation #18.1: Circles of Connection

Breathe and relax. Place your body in a comfortable position. Deepen the breath. Allow thoughts and tensions to dissolve. As you breathe and soften with each breath, draw breath into your heart. **Draw in love, sending it to your immediate circle.** Cultivate feelings of empathic love and compassion. Draw in love from the cosmos and the Earth. Spread all of this love from your heart into your most immediate circle, such as close family and friends and beloved pets.

Expand the love. Continue to breathe slowly and deeply, and spread the love and positive energy to your community. "Community" may be the local area you live in, or the tribal groups you align with, like organizations or people you work with, your yoga community, meditation sangha, and other like-minded groups.

As you continue to breathe and the power of loving intention builds, send the next waves to your geographical region. Expand to breathe love outwardly to your country and then beyond, moving your breath in ever-widening circles throughout the planet. Include plants, animals and the Earth herself. Notice if you can see or feel a connection with conscious beings living throughout the world, who are also sending out their intent for love, peace and healing. There is a layer of Light and positive intent that has been growing and thickening over the past decades. Breathe this in and remember the power of group intention. From here, if you wish, you can continue to widen the circle to include other planets, life-forms and galaxies, until you are breathing love throughout infinity, and feeling love returned right back to you.

2. Journal Reflection: Your Role in the World

1. List in your journal all the ways you feel you are currently connected and of service to your community and the world.

2. Write down the actions you'd like to take to be more aligned with both inner peace and healing that would ripple out to the world. Include the direct actions you'd like to take to help the healing and transformation process.

3. As you look at your two lists, consider if you'd like to make any changes in the near future. Then repeat the affirmation with a soft and loving heart: "I am enough. I do enough." What comes up for you? Can you contemplate actions you'd like to take to connect with the world and be part of needed changes *and also* be in acceptance with the way you are and how life is, without necessarily having to change anything at all?

CHAPTER NINETEEN

Everyday Awakening: (Infinite) Soul Path

*"You must understand the whole of life, not just one little
part of it. That is why you must read, that is why you must
look at the skies, that is why you must sing and dance,
and write poems and suffer and understand, for all that is life."*
—Jiddu Krishnamurti

Each day we have a choice to be awake and alive—or stumble
blindly down well-worn paths, on autopilot, lost in cultural
beliefs and conditioning.

"Everyday awakening" is an attitude adjustment, the natural
result of spiritual exploration, understanding and practice.

Many don't ask the deeper questions about the meaning of
life until it is too late. Death is hovering. Who wants to be the
person who looks at their life in the rearview mirror and finds it
a treadmill of work with no significant heartfelt purpose? Or find

that you accomplished a major goal but missed the beauty and joy in random moments?

The solution is to ponder life, understand your values and soul path, and then to let it all sit in the background as awareness. You know who you are and why you're here. Now, how does that translate moment to moment? If you believe your path is to become the healer of the world, but you're impatient and frustrated at every turn throughout the day, you're not living congruently. You're not even living enjoyably.

To live fully, we must also be aware that death comes too. We can be filled with fear about death, or facing this reality can encourage us to live fully while we're here. Years of talking to spirits has convinced me that life is ongoing and that we truly drop our bodies and still maintain a sense of self on the other side. We really do go to the Light, and continue to cherish those left behind, even when the human relationship wasn't quite so easy.

Perhaps the many offerings and viewpoints of this book have given you a fresh vision, a road map to guide you.

You now have a soul path mission statement and manageable subgoals. You have looked at your life from the perspectives of spirit, body and mind/emotion. Perhaps you can feel reverence and excitement about the beauty of your path or simply in having more clarity. Hopefully you can also hold the awareness that you are perfect and there's ultimately nothing to do but live, meeting each moment's manifestations as they arise. Can you hold the soul path intentions and goals like butterflies resting lightly on your fingertips?

You have multiple choices about attitude and awareness in each simple moment throughout the day. You are more likely to feel you're thriving if your mundane time is infused with conscious, if not sacred, awareness. If each thought, word and action is creating the future, attentiveness to words and actions you might normally take without much thought is important. What words do you choose? What is the emotional tone that permeates your interactions? Are you in alignment with truth while checking out at the grocery store? Are you in love with the world while brushing your teeth?

A goal of living mindfully is a whole lot easier if we can create a slightly slower life pace than most of us experience today.

There's an island in Greece where the residents live to be very old. There are many other cultures around the world with high levels of centenarians too, but this story from the Greek island of Ikaria is particularly fascinating.

Stamatis Moraitis came to the United States in 1943 for treatment of a war injury. He settled down, raised a family, and in 1976 was diagnosed with lung cancer. With a grim forecast of nine months to live, he moved back to his home, Ikaria. He imagined a funeral would be cheaper there. Bedridden at first, he slept a lot, ate the local food and was visited by friends and family. Slowly he began to feel better. As he gained strength he immersed himself in the local life, including living simply and eating wild greens, otherwise known as weeds. He walked and gardened, napped and socialized. Perhaps you can guess the outcome. Months turned into years and he became healthier and healthier, and now after more than three decades of simple, carefree life, he is close to one hundred years old and has no cancer at all.

Can we all move to a Greek island, or to the Himalayas, or an island off the coast of Japan? No, probably not. Yet we can live simpler, more balanced, healthier lives. We can choose to cultivate strong, spiritually-centered values.

The Yamas and Niyamas of traditional yoga philosophy are one way to provide context for daily spiritual contemplation. Each one of these ten rules or observances is simple, subtle and yet also complex. You can pick one and meditate on it every day for months and still find new perspectives on your self and your motivations. To understand these concepts in a way that is adapted to our modern life, I highly recommend the book, *The*

Yamas and Niyamas: Exploring Yoga's Ethical Practice by Deborah Adele.

Yamas are the attitudes or disciplined choices we contemplate for relationships with others.

1. Non-harming (Ahimsa) suggests that we strive to do no harm to others. This requires us to come into a compassionate inner power and consider nuanced choices. At the simplest level, we don't hurt other people directly or indirectly. Many believe this means we need to be vegetarian or vegan to not harm animals. Often the blind spots are found in the ways we harm ourselves through our unexamined choices. I love the contemplation of Ahimsa as it relates to yoga or physical exercise. Often we are hurting our own bodies as we power through something we "think" is good for us.

2. Truth (Satya) asks us to ponder honesty in daily life. Although many of us might claim to be honest people, truth can be slippery and includes non-truth by omission or not being honest with ourselves. Truth must also be modified by the goal of not harming others; in relationship we find a way to speak truth with care and without harm.

3. Non-stealing (Asteya) suggests we choose to live with integrity and don't take what is not ours. Beyond the obvious of not shoplifting or taking others' possessions, we can look at the ways we siphon energy from others or take too many resources from the Earth. If you take a bite of someone else's food without asking, if you use your friend's moisturizers—simple unexamined choices—are you out of alignment with Asteya?

4. Non-excess (Brahmacharya) teaches us to live simply in moderate balance with our needs, not taking too much. Although this Yama has been sometimes construed as urging celibacy, Yamas only ask that we consider what is truthfully balanced for us and in relationship to our time of life. We can ponder Brahmacharya as we choose between excess or moderation in food selection, work habits, sexuality, or any other choice where we are between a sense of the sacred and the ego desire for excess consumption.

5. Non-possessiveness or grasping (Aparigraha) suggests that we live lightly on this planet, releasing attachment again and again. Can you simplify your life and let go of all you don't actually need? Can you release attachment whenever you notice it, relaxing more gently into life arising?

Niyamas are concepts to ponder about the way we treat ourselves. These are personal care and conscious living choices. In *The Heart of Yoga*, another one of my favorite books, T.K.V. Desikachar says, "Compared with the Yamas, the Niyamas are more intimate and personal."

1. Cleanliness (Saucha): This asks us to treat ourselves with respect, to maintain cleanliness inside our body and on the outside, to maintain purity in our mind too. This might include a physical yoga practice or even simple luxurious stretches and consciously deep, slow breaths. Purification practices, detoxing, massaging your body with oil and a daily clean diet are other possible choices in alignment with Saucha.

2. Contentment (Santosha): In each moment we have a choice to be content and accepting of life as it arises

or to be in struggle. As we observe our resistance and choose gratitude and contentment, life flows. To meditate on contentment asks us to choose to be content as an act of will when the ego prefers to stay stuck in likes and dislikes. The ego/mind judges endlessly, creating emotional ripples about inconsequential events. Santosha softens this particular mind-wheel.

3.   Self-Discipline (Tapas); This is the choice to place ourselves in the fire of transformation, accepting all challenging events and all beings as teachers. Here we cultivate the attitude of not grasping so tightly to the desire that all life experiences be easy. Every event in life is part of a deep, transformative process, offering the fruits of past thought, word and action.

4.   Self-Study (Svadhyaya): The process of self-examination is a fruitful part of a daily, life-affirming, awakening practice. If you've read this book all the way through and worked with the exercises, you've been cultivating self-study in a deep, thorough way. Every day we have an opportunity to be in a process of self-study or to simply float through life unaware. The consciousness can be simple; keep eyes open. See. Feel. Be.

5.   Surrender (Ishvara Pranidhana). However you conceive of the divine force of life, to surrender to that which rests in the heart of all matter takes the focus away from ego self and toward a higher power. Surrender is the keyword of Pisces, the culmination of the zodiac. When we align with the cosmos, we submit to the journey of both loss and magic. The potential for loss, magic and everything in between is always there, whether we surrender to it or not. With surrender we participate in life with fluidity and grace.

OTHER VALUES:

You can work with the Ten Commandments or any other principles with which you feel aligned. Integrity is very personal; you know when you're stepping on your own values. You'll usually feel a vague sense of discomfort in the belly. You can make a list of your personal values: love, compassion, devotion, excellence, witnessing, unity, faith and trust . . . Your list could be long and unique. Choose a word to anchor your daily mindfulness practice and live with that word and all it means to you until the concept has permeated your consciousness.

Consider working with one concept at a time for at least thirty days; ninety days allows for a more thorough reflection. This ethical value meditation will allow you to you notice things about yourself and your attitudes and actions that never occurred to you before. There is a quiet, inner richness to exploring life through these words and concepts.

What matters to you? You could spend a lifetime contemplating love and honoring self-love, compassion, empathy and love for others in every conscious moment.

You get to choose the attitude that envelops you on this stroll down the lane of life. What will it be?

As we embrace a mindful daily life, we slow down just a bit. Simple interactions become more interesting. The mind can become focused on what you are doing in this moment with all of its layers and nuance. The tendency to project blame onto others (or the universe) is lessened, the dramas less interesting. Awareness (that which is you, viewing from High Self) contemplates if you spoke truth as you know it, and if you were able to do so without harm. It's interesting, not judgmental. The goal is simply to be aligned with higher principles, slowing yourself down so the ego/mind habit patterns are no longer in control. You create space to live in accord with your path, clear that you are a Spirit being having a physical expression.

ONE LAST THING: DAILY SPACE

As you have defined your intentions, have you left time for space—to lie on the bed and look at the clouds through a window, to feel music stream through your cells, to pet a furry friend or to giggle with a child? We all need time to "be" scattered throughout the days of a soul-infused life.

It's all about balance.

You have clarified your soul path in a myriad of ways. This is an empowering act. As you take even small steps toward your goals, you will feel aligned and purposeful. The excess, habit-infused patterns dissolve and fall away.

Now give yourself lots of breathing space to modify, reconsider, relax, play and live with an open heart. This is truly the best attitude to allow the flow and abundance of the universe to find you.

May you be aligned with your unique Soul Path
to express authentic Spirit in each breath.

#19 - REFLECTION

1. Journal Reflection: The End leads to the Beginning
1. Choose a Yama, Niyama or a value concept word to work with for the next ninety days. Read about it, focus on the word in meditation and observe yourself in relation to this concept in your daily interactions. Allow awareness to deepen and evolve with very little effort.
2. Take the "after" photo of your life. How have you integrated the Four Pillars of Healing in your day-to-day life? Take a moment to be grateful for all that you have.
3. Be flexible. Allow your Soul Path Way to evolve and change with deeper, richer and more nuanced understanding of who you are and what this precious life is all about.

A LIST OF PROMINENT
EVOLUTIONARY ASTROLOGERS

Virginia Bell, New York, NY
www.virginiabellastrology.com

Maurice Fernandez
www.mauricefernandez.com
His website includes a directory of astrologers he's trained.

Hadley Fitzgerald, Sherman Oaks, CA
www.eternityroad.com

Steven Forrest
www.forrestastrology.com
Forrest-trained astrologers can be found here:
www.forrestastrology.com/forrest-trained-astrologers

Sheri Horn Hasan, Marlboro, NJ
www.karmicevolution.com

Amy Herring, Seattle, WA
www.heavenlytruth.com

Tom Jacobs, Tucson, AZ
www.tdjacobs.com

Mark Jones
www.plutoschool.com

Alice Loffredo
www.astrologykarmaandyou.com

Rose Marcus
www.rosemarcus.com

Kim Marie
www.evolutionaryastrology.net
For evolutionary astrologers in the Jeffrey Green lineage.

Jessica Shepherd, Fairfax, CA
www.moonkissd.com

Kay Taylor, Emeryville & Berkeley, CA
www.kaytaylor.com
Soul Path practitioners are trained in evolutionary astrology, in-
tuition and/or psychosynthesis:
www.kaytaylor.com/soul-path-practitioners

Patricia Walsh
www.HealThePast.com

Additional Resources
The website FindAnAstrologer.com has a searchable database of astrologers and you can search for "evolutionary astrology" as a specialty.

TABLE OF NODES

Date From	Date To	South Node Sign	People You Know
Aug 16, 1919	Feb 7, 1921	Taurus	
Feb 8, 1921	Aug 22, 1922	Aries	
Aug 23, 1922	Aug 27, 1922	Pisces	
Aug 28, 1922	Aug 31, 1922	Aries	
Sept 1, 1922	Apr 22, 1924	Pisces	
Apr 23, 1924	Oct 26, 1925	Aquarius	
Oct 27, 1925	Apr 16, 1927	Capricorn	
Apr 17, 1927	Dec 28, 1928	Sagittarius	
Dec 29, 1928	Jul 7, 1930	Scorpio	
Jul 8, 1930	Dec 28, 1931	Libra	
Dec 29, 1928	July 7, 1930	Virgo	
Jul 25, 1933	Mar 8, 1935	Leo	
Mar 9, 1935	Sept 14, 1936	Cancer	
Sept 15, 1936	Mar 3, 1938	Gemini	
Mar 4, 1938	Sept 11, 1939	Taurus	
Sept 12, 1939	May 24, 1941	Aries	
May 25, 1941	Nov 21, 1942	Pisces	
Nov 22, 1942	May 11, 1944	Aquarius	
May 12, 1944	Dec 3, 1945	Capricorn	
Dec 4, 1945	Aug 2, 1947	Sagittarius	
Aug 3, 1947	Jan 26, 1949	Scorpio	
Jan 27, 1949	Jul 26, 1950	Libra	

Date From	Date To	South Node Sign	People You Know
Jul 27, 1950	Mar 28, 1952	Virgo	
Mar 29, 1952	Oct 9, 1953	Leo	
Oct 10, 1953	Apr 2, 1955	Cancer	
Apr 3, 1955	Oct 4, 1956	Gemini	
Oct 5, 1956	Jun 16, 1958	Taurus	
Jun 17, 1958	Dec 15, 1959	Aries	
Dec 16, 1959	Jun 10, 1961	Pisces	
June 11, 1961	Dec 23, 1963	Aquarius	
Dec 24, 1962	Aug 25, 1964	Capricorn	
Aug 26 1964	Feb 19, 1966	Sagittarius	
Feb 20, 1966	Aug 19, 1967	Scorpio	
Aug 20, 1967	Apr 19, 1969	Libra	
Apr 20, 1969	Nov 2, 1970	Virgo	
Nov 3, 1970	Apr 27, 1972	Leo	
Apr 28, 1972	Oct 27, 1973	Cancer	
Oct 28, 1973	Jul 9, 1975	Gemini	
Jul 10, 1975	Jan 7, 1977	Taurus	
Jan 8, 1977	Jul 5, 1978	Aries	
Jul 6, 1978	Jan 5, 1980	Pisces	
Jan 6, 1980	Sept 24, 1981	Aquarius	
Sept 25, 1981	Mar 16, 1983	Capricorn	
Mar 17, 1983	Sept 11, 1984	Sagittarius	
Sept 12, 1984	Apr 6, 1986	Scorpio	
Apr 7, 1986	May 5, 1986	Libra	
May 6, 1986	May 8, 1986	Scorpio	
May 9, 1986	Dec 2, 1987	Libra	
Dec 3, 1987	May 22, 1989	Virgo	
May 23, 1989	Nov 18, 1990	Leo	

Date From	Date To	South Node Sign	People You Know
Nov 19, 1990	Aug 1, 1992	Cancer	
Aug 2, 1992	Feb 1, 1994	Gemini	
Feb 2, 1994	Jul 31, 1995	Taurus	
Aug 1, 1995	Jan 25, 1997	Aries	
Jan 26, 1997	Oct 20, 1998	Pisces	
Oct 21, 1998	Apr 9, 2000	Aquarius	
April 10, 2000	Oct 13, 2001	Capricorn	
Oct 14, 2001	Apr 14, 2003	Sagittarius	
Apr 15, 2003	Dec 26, 2004	Scorpio	
Dec 27, 2004	June 22, 2006	Libra	
Jun 23, 2006	Dec 18, 2007	Virgo	
Dec 19, 2007	Aug 21, 2009	Leo	
Aug 22, 2009	Mar 3, 2011	Cancer	
Mar 4, 2011	Aug 29, 2012	Gemini	
Aug 29, 2012	Feb 18, 2014	Taurus	
Feb 19, 2014	Nov 11, 2015	Aries	
Nov 12, 2015	May 9, 2017	Pisces	
May 10, 2017	Nov 6, 2018	Aquarius	
Nov 7, 2018	May 5, 2020	Capricorn	
May 6, 2020	Jan 18, 2022	Sagittarius	
Jan 19, 2022	Jul 17, 2023	Scorpio	
July 18, 2023	Jan 11, 2025	Libra	

PLUTO TABLE

*Remember to double check with astrological software
if your birthday is near a changing date.*

Pluto in

Cancer	May 26, 1914 to June 14, 1939
Leo	June 14, 1939 to August 19, 1957
Virgo	August 19, 1957 to October 5, 1971
	April 17, 1972 to July 30, 1972
Libra	October 5, 1971 to April 17, 1972
	July 30, 1972 to November 5, 1983
Scorpio	November 5, 1983 to May 18, 1984
	August 2, 1984 to January 17, 1995
	April 21, 1995 to November 10, 1995
Sagittarius	January 17, 1995 to April 20, 1995
	November 10, 1995 to January 27, 2008
	June 13, 2008 to November 26, 2008
Capricorn	January 25, 2008 to June 13, 2008
	November 26, 2008 to March 23, 2023
	June 11, 2023 to January 20, 2024
Aquarius	March 23, 2023 to June 11, 2023
	January 20, 2024 to September 1, 2024
	November 19, 2024 to March 8, 2043
	August 31, 2043 to January 19, 2044

SATURN TABLE
(EASTERN TIMES)

Remember to check astrological software to find your
Saturn placement if your birthday is near a changing time.

Oct 7, 1921	12:22 PM Saturn enters Libra
Dec 19, 1923	11:25 PM Saturn enters Scorpio
Apr 6, 1924	3:35 AM Saturn Rx enters Libra
Sep 13, 1924	6:00 PM Saturn enters Scorpio
Dec 2, 1926	5:35 PM Saturn enters Sagittarius
Mar 15, 1929	8:49 AM Saturn enters Capricorn
May 5, 1929	12:18 AM Saturn Rx enters Sagittarius
Nov 29, 1929	11:22 PM Saturn enters Capricorn
Feb 23, 1932	9:47 PM Saturn enters Aquarius
Aug 13, 1932	7:14 AM Saturn Rx enters Capricorn
Nov 19, 1932	9:10 PM Saturn enters Aquarius
Feb 14, 1935	9:08 AM Saturn enters Pisces
Apr 25, 1937	2:29 AM Saturn enters Aries
Oct 17, 1937	10:41 PM Saturn Rx enters Pisces
Jan 14, 1938	5:31 AM Saturn enters Aries
Jul 6, 1939	1:45 AM Saturn enters Taurus
Sep 22, 1939	1:18 AM Saturn Rx enters Aries
Mar 20, 1940	4:40 AM Saturn enters Taurus
May 8, 1942	3:39 PM Saturn enters Gemini
Jun 20, 1944	3:48 AM Saturn enters Cancer
Aug 2, 1946	10:42 AM Saturn enters Leo
Sep 19, 1948	12:36 AM Saturn enters Virgo
Apr 2, 1949	10:38 PM Saturn Rx enters Leo

May 29, 1949	8:59 AM Saturn enters Virgo
Nov 20, 1950	10:50 AM Saturn enters Libra
Mar 7, 1951	7:12 AM Saturn Rx enters Virgo
Aug 13, 1951	12:44 PM Saturn enters Libra
Oct 22, 1953	10:36 AM Saturn enters Scorpio
Jan 12, 1956	1:46 PM Saturn enters Sagittarius
May 13, 1956	11:45 PM Saturn Rx enters Scorpio
Oct 10, 1956	10:11 AM Saturn enters Sagittarius
Jan 5, 1959	8:33 AM Saturn enters Capricorn
Jan 3, 1962	2:01 PM Saturn enters Aquarius
Mar 23, 1964	11:18 PM Saturn enters Pisces
Sep 16, 1964	5:04 PM Saturn Rx enters Aquarius
Dec 16, 1964	12:39 AM Saturn enters Pisces
Mar 3, 1967	4:32 PM Saturn enters Aries
Apr 29, 1969	6:23 PM Saturn enters Taurus
Jun 18, 1971	12:09 PM Saturn enters Gemini
Jan 9, 1972	10:43 PM Saturn Rx enters Taurus
Feb 21, 1972	9:52 AM Saturn enters Gemini
Aug 1, 1973	6:20 PM Saturn enters Cancer
Jan 7, 1974	3:26 PM Saturn Rx enters Gemini
Apr 18, 1974	5:34 PM Saturn enters Cancer
Sep 17, 1975	12:57 AM Saturn enters Leo
Jan 14, 1976	8:16 AM Saturn Rx enters Cancer
Jun 5, 1976	1:09 AM Saturn enters Leo
Nov 16, 1977	9:43 PM Saturn enters Virgo
Jan 4, 1978	7:44 PM Saturn Rx enters Leo
Jul 26, 1978	8:02 AM Saturn enters Virgo
Sep 21, 1980	6:48 AM Saturn enters Libra
Nov 29, 1982	5:29 AM Saturn enters Scorpio
May 6, 1983	3:29 PM Saturn Rx enters Libra
Aug 24, 1983	7:54 AM Saturn enters Scorpio
Nov 16, 1985	9:10 PM Saturn enters Sagittarius
Feb 13, 1988	6:51 PM Saturn enters Capricorn
Jun 10, 1988	1:22 AM Saturn Rx enters Sagittarius

Nov 12, 1988	4:26 AM Saturn enters Capricorn
Feb 6, 1991	1:51 PM Saturn enters Aquarius
May 21, 1993	12:58 AM Saturn enters Pisces
Jun 30, 1993	4:29 AM Saturn Rx enters Aquarius
Jan 28, 1994	6:43 PM Saturn enters Pisces
Apr 7, 1996	4:49 AM Saturn enters Aries
Jun 9, 1998	2:07 AM Saturn enters Taurus
Oct 25, 1998	1:41 PM Saturn Rx enters Aries
Feb 28, 1999	8:26 PM Saturn enters Taurus
Aug 9, 2000	10:26 PM Saturn enters Gemini
Oct 15, 2000	8:44 PM Saturn Rx enters Taurus
Apr 20, 2001	5:59 PM Saturn enters Gemini
Jul 12, 2001	8:03 PM Jupiter enters Cancer
Jun 3, 2003	9:28 PM Saturn enters Cancer
Jul 16, 2005	8:31 AM Saturn enters Leo
Sep 2, 2007	9:49 AM Saturn enters Virgo
Oct 29, 2009	1:09 PM Saturn enters Libra
Apr 7, 2010	2:51 PM Saturn Rx enters Virgo
Jul 21, 2010	11:10 AM Saturn enters Libra
Apr 7, 2010	2:51 PM Saturn Rx enters Virgo
Jul 21, 2010	11:10 AM Saturn enters Libra
Oct 5, 2012	4:34 PM Saturn enters Scorpio
Dec 23, 2014	11:34 AM Saturn enters Sagittarius
Jun 14, 2015	8:36 PM Saturn Rx enters Scorpio
Sep 17, 2015	10:49 PM Saturn enters Sagittarius
Dec 19, 2017	11:49 PM Saturn enters Capricorn
Mar 21, 2020	11:58 PM Saturn enters Aquarius
Jul 1, 2020	7:37 PM Saturn Rx enters Capricorn
Dec 17, 2020	12:04 AM Saturn enters Aquarius
Mar 7, 2023	8:34 AM Saturn enters Pisces
May 24, 2025	11:35 PM Saturn enters Aries
Sep 1, 2025	4:06 AM Saturn Rx enters Pisces
Feb 13, 2026	7:11 PM Saturn enters Aries
Apr 12, 2028	11:39 PM Saturn enters Taurus

May 31, 2030	10:34 PM Saturn enters Gemini
Jul 13, 2032	10:16 PM Saturn enters Cancer
Aug 26, 2034	10:46 PM Saturn enters Leo
Feb 15, 2035	2:34 PM Saturn Rx enters Cancer
May 11, 2035	4:44 PM Saturn enters Leo
Oct 16, 2036	3:34 AM Saturn enters Virgo
Feb 11, 2037	1:46 AM Saturn Rx enters Leo
Jul 6, 2037	10:30 PM Saturn enters Virgo
Sep 5, 2039	11:14 AM Saturn enters Libra
Nov 11, 2041	5:57 AM Saturn enters Scorpio
Jun 21, 2042	6:26 AM Saturn Rx enters Libra
Jul 14, 2042	9:58 AM Saturn enters Scorpio
Feb 21, 2044	9:20 AM Saturn enters Sagittarius
Mar 25, 2044	6:02 AM Saturn Rx enters Scorpio
Oct 31, 2044	8:51 AM Saturn enters Sagittarius

REFLECTIONS:
TABLE OF MEDITATIONS
& JOURNAL EXERCISES

Chapter 1   1. Meditation #1.1: Lemon Exercise
               2. Meditation #1.2: The Crossroads
               3. Soul Path Offering

Chapter 2   1. Meditation #2.1: Lifescan for
                  Soul Path Memories
               2. Journal Reflection on Memories
                  & Life Moments

Chapter 3   1. Journal Reflection on Twelve Areas of Life

Chapter 4   1. Journal Reflection on the Nodes
               2. Meditation #4.1: Nodal Integration

Chapter 5   1. Journal Reflection on Pluto

Chapter 6   1. Journal Reflection on Saturn

Chapter 7   1. Journal Reflection on Soul Path Mission

Chapter 8   1. Journal Reflection on Refining
                  the Soul Path Mission
               2. Journal Reflection on Four
                  Pillars of Healing
               3. Meditation #8.1: Feeling All Four Pillars

Chapter 9   1. Journal Reflection on What
               is Asked of Me Now?
              2. Journal Reflection on Connection to Spirit
              3. Journal Reflection on Spirit
               & Mission Statement

Chapter 10   1. Meditation: setting up a regular practice

Chapter 11   1. Meditation #11.1: To run energy
               and create boundaries
              2. Meditation #11.2: To cleanse the chakras
              3. Meditation #11.3: To connect
               with your spirit guide
              4. Meditation #11.4: To connect with
               heart energy: pink & green
              5. Journal Reflection:
               Clairsentience & Empathy
              6. Journal Reflection:
               Clairaudience & Telepathy
              7. Journal Reflection: Clairvoyance & Vision
              8. Journal Reflection: Channeling

Chapter 12   1. Meditation #12.1: Zen: the
               style of simplicity
              2. Soul Path Offering: Thought
               Mindfulness & Positive Thinking
              3. Journal Reflection: Thoughts & Beliefs

Chapter 13   1. Meditation #13.1: Emotion
              2. Meditation #13.2: Release
               Emotion in Water
              3. Meditation #13.3: Subpersonality Process
              4. Journal Reflection on Emotion

Chapter 14   1. Soul Path Offering: Massage
2. Soul Path Offering: Savasana Nap
3. Meditation #14.1: Purify Space
4. Soul Path Offering: Walk
    with Your Inner Child
5. Journal Reflection: Mission & Action

Chapter 15   1. Soul Path Offering: Creation Steps
2. Meditation #15.1: Meditation
    for Resistant Subpersonality
3. Meditation #15.2: Meditation to
    Release Emotional Blockage
4. Soul Path Offering: Burn & Release
5. Meditation #15.3: Forgiveness Meditation

Chapter 16   1. Journal Reflection: Your
    Unique Daily Plan

Chapter 17   1. Journal Reflection: Beloveds & Tribe
2. Meditation #17.1: Circle of Hearts
3. Soul Path Offering: Manifesting Circle

Chapter 18   1. Meditation #18.1: Circles of Connection
2. Journal Reflection: Your Role in the World

Chapter 19   1. Journal Reflection: The End
    leads to the Beginning

BIBLIOGRAPHY
Recommended Reading

Adele, Deborah. *The Yamas & Niyamas.*
Adyashanti. *Falling into Grace.*
————. *The Way of Liberation.*
Assagioli, Roberto. *Psychosynthesis.*
Baldwin, William, J. *Spirit Releasement Therapy: A Technique Manual.*
Bogart, Greg. *Astrology and Meditation.*
————. *Astrology and Spiritual Awakening.*
————. *Dreamwork and Self-Healing: Unfolding the Symbols of the Unconscious.*
————. *Planets in Therapy.*
————. *Therapeutic Astrology.*
Brown, Molly Young. *Unfolding Self: The Practice of Psychosynthesis.*
Chodron, Pema. *Start Where You Are.*
————. *When Things Fall Apart.*
Chopra, Deepak. *The Seven Spiritual Laws of Success.*
Desikachar, T.K.V. *The Heart of Yoga.*
Dominguez, Joe & Vicki Robin. *Your Money or Your Life.*
Dooley, Mike. *Leveraging the Universe.*
Duggan, William. *Strategic Intuition.*
Fernandez, Maurice. *Astrology & the Evolution of Consciousness Volume One.*
Firman, John & Ann Gila. *A Psychotherapy of Love.*
————. *The Primal Wound.*
————. *Psychosynthesis: A Psychology of the Spirit.*

Forrest, Steven: *The Book of Neptune.*
———. *The Book of Pluto.*
———. *The Changing Sky.*
———. *The Inner Sky.*
———. *Yesterday's Sky.*
Gendlin, Eugene. *Focusing.*
Hay, Louise. *You Can Heal Your Life.*
Helliwell & Huang study (2013)
http://journals.plos.org/plosone/article?id=10.1371/journal.
    pone.0072754
Hicks, Esther & Jerry. *The Law of Attraction: The Basics of the
    Teachings of Abraham.*
Hillman, James. *The Soul's Code.*
Idemon, Richard. *The Magic Thread.*
———. *Through the Looking Glass*
Klein, Gary. *The Power of Intuition: How to Use your Gut Feelings
    to Make Decisions at Work.*
Kondo, Marie. *The Life-Changing Magic of Tidying Up.*
Lutin, Michael. *SunShines: The Astrology of Being Happy.*
Pessoa, Luiz. *The Cognitive-Emotional Brain: From Interactions
    to Integration.*
Ponder, Catherine. *The Dynamic Laws of Prosperity.*
Roth, Geneen. *When Food is Love.*
Simpkins, Kimber. *Full.*
Small, Jacquelyn. *Awakening in Time.*
Stanford Study on Walking in Nature: https://news.stanford.
    edu/2015/06/30/hiking-mental-health-063015/
Stevenson, Ian. *Children Who Remember Previous Lives.*
Strom, Max. *A Life Worth Breathing.*
Trungpa, Chogyam. *Cutting Through Spiritual Materialism.*
Wallace, Amy and Bill Henkin. *The Psychic Healing Book.*
Wallis, Christopher D. *Tantra Illuminated*
Welwood, John. *Toward a Psychology of Awakening.*
Wiseman, Richard. *The Luck Factor.*

ABOUT THE AUTHOR

Kay Taylor is a beloved visionary guide, healer and teacher who has cultivated her inspiring synthesis of wisdom teachings for more than three decades.

A natural clairvoyant and empath since childhood, Kay weaves many healing threads into her life's work including astrology, psychosynthesis (a spiritual psychology), hypnotherapy, psychic healing arts, bodywork and yoga. Her teachings are infused with empathy and gentle humor born of many challenging life experiences.

Over the years Kay has taught thousands of individuals how to develop their intuitive, astrological and counseling skills from novice to the professional level. She leads retreats and workshops throughout the world and lectures at professional astrology conferences. Kay is an ISAR (International Society for Astrological Research) CAP certified astrologer and Consulting Skills trainer and is NCGR (National Council for Geocosmic Research) Level II certified. She wrote for Astrology.com for many years and was a featured writer in the OPA (Organization for Professional Astrology) anthology The Professional Astrologer. Before committing fully to her soul path, she obtained an MBA in Finance.

Kay resides in the SF Bay area. Information about private sessions, retreats and training can be found at www.kaytaylor.com.